with warmest wishes,

Margaret Bennett

Dìleab Ailein

Margaret Bennett was brought up in a family of Scottish tradition bearers, Gaelic on her mother's side (from Skye) and Lowland Scots on her father's. Singer, storyteller, folklorist, writer, and broadcaster, recipient of the *Master Music Maker Award* (USA) and *Celtic Women International Award* (USA/Canada) for "lifelong service to Scottish Culture", she is widely regarded as "Scotland's foremost folklorist".

Her books include *The Last Stronghold: Scottish Gaelic Traditions in Newfoundland*, (1989, awarded the Ruth Michaelis-Jena Ratchliff Folklore prize), *Oatmeal and the Catechism: Scottish Gaelic Settlers in Quebec*, (1998 and 2004, winner of the Société historique du Canada Clio Award), and bestseller *Scottish Customs from the Cradle to the Grave*, (1992 and 2004). Musical collaborations with her late son, Martyn, feature in theatre and film, (including the internationally acclaimed production, 'The Black Watch').

As the late Hamish Henderson wrote, "Margaret embodies the spirit of Scotland."

OTHER BOOKS BY THE AUTHOR

'It's not the Time You Have …' Notes and Memories of Music-making with Martyn Bennett

'See When You Look Back …' Clydeside Reminiscences of the Home Front, 1939—45, Glasgow

'Then Another Thing ...' Remembered in Perthshire, with Doris Rougvie

EDITED WORK–'Recollections of an Argyllshire Drover' & Other West Highland Chronicles by Eric R. Cregeen

RECORDINGS

'In the Sunny Long Ago '; 'Glen Lyon–a song cycle'; 'Take the Road to Aberfeldy' and 'Love and Loss'–Remembering Martyn in Scotland's Music

The Legacy of Allan MacArthur
Dìleab Ailein
Newfoundland Traditions Across Four Generations

Margaret Bennett

Scottish Folklore Collection
Codroy Valley, Newfoundland, 1969–2009

GRACE NOTE PUBLICATIONS

Dìleab Ailein
A' chiad fhoillseachadh an 2009 le
GRACE NOTE PUBLICATIONS CIC
Grange of Locherlour
Uachdar Tìre mu Chraoibh
Siorrachd Pheairt PH7 4JS, ALBA
Post-dealain: gonzalo@gracenotereading.co.uk

LAGE/ISBN 978-0-9552326-8-8

Dh'fhoillsich Grace Note Publications an leabhar seo
an co-bhuinn ri Grace Notes Scotland (SC040434)
Carthannas Clàraichte an Alba

Tha clàradh CIP dhan leabhar seo ri fhaighinn bho Leabharlann Bhreatainn.

Fhuaireadh taic rannsachaidh bho

RSAMD
*The ROYAL SCOTTISH ACADEMY
of MUSIC & DRAMA*

Foundation for Canadian
Studies in the UK

Chuidich Comhairle nan Leabhraichean am foillsichear
le cosgaisean an leabhair seo.

Bhon chaill mi a' Ghàidhlig na b' fheàrr cha d' fhuair mi
Since I've lost Gaelic, nothing better have I found

ALLAN MACARTHUR

Dedication

To the memory of **Allan MacArthur (1884—1971)**,
whose inspirational legacy comes from his unfailing loyalty to the
language and traditional culture of his own people; and to that of his wife,
Mary (MacDonald) MacArthur (1896—1975), who radiated
kindness and wisdom in her companionship.

&

To my son, **Martyn Bennett (1971—2005)**,
who listened to every detail, sharing Allan MacArthur's passion for
the culture they loved. His imaginative compositions and inspired
musical performances honour the past while creating a wonderful
legacy for the future.

Cuimhneachan

Mar chuimhneachan air **Ailean MacArtair (1884—1971)**,
a dh'fhàg dìleab bhrosnachail mar thoradh air a dhìlseachd do
chànan is do dhualchas a dhaoine fhèin; agus cuideachd air a bhean,
Màiri (Dhòmhnallach) NicArtair (1896—1975), a bha na companach
coibhneil, glic.

&

Mo mhac, **Martyn Bennett (1971—2005)**,
a dh'èist gu mionaideach agus a bha cho measail air an
dualchas ri Ailean MacArtair. Tha an obair mhac-meanmnach
a sgrìobh e agus a chluich bhrosnachail a' toirt urram dhan
àm a dh'fhalbh agus nan dìleab iongantach dhan àm ri teachd.

CD 1

MacArthur's Cèilidh Cèilidh MhicArtair

CD 2

MacArthur's Kitchen Party Partaidh Cidsin Mhic Artair

Introduction

Here's a health to the traveller who left Scotland!

For the traveller crossing the Atlantic on a northern route from Scotland to North America, the first sighting of land is Newfoundland. For Scottish emigrants of the eighteenth and nineteenth centuries, however, it was not the first port of call, particularly for Highlanders exiled during the infamous Clearances, that began in the 1740s and lasted till the late nineteenth century. 'The Rock', as some affectionately call the island, was settled in the seventeenth century by Irish, English and French fishermen harvesting codfish. The Irish knew it as '*talamh an èisg*' —land of the codfish—as it was the currency of the island for centuries. To this day, strong influences of all three peoples can be heard in tunes and instrumental styles, songs and speech patterns and can be seen in dances. Less well known, however, is the history or folklore of the Scots who now make up a mere one percent of Newfoundland's population.

The Codroy Valley on the west coast became the final destination for a close-knit group of Gaelic-speaking immigrants who came, not for the lucrative fishing, but simply for a piece of land on which to make a living. Official histories of their time give little or no detail about them or their experiences, but they themselves kept alive their history, culture and Gaelic traditions for several generations. Today, the common language is English, but if you visit the Valley you can still sense the Scottish Gaelic influences in the way of life, as well as in the music, songs, and dances.

Ro-ràdh

Deoch-slàinte a' chuairteir a ghluais à Albainn!

A' dol tarsainn Cuan an Antlantaig tuath bho Alba gu Ameireaga a Tuath, 's e An Talamh Ùr a' chiad fhearann a chithear. Ach cha b' e seo a' chiad phort air am biodh eilthirich à Alba san ochdamh agus san naoidheamh linn deug a' tadhal. Bha seo gu h-àraidh fìor mu na Gàidheil a chaidh fhògradh aig àm nam Fuadaichean a thòisich sna 1740 an agus a lean gu faisg air deireadh an naoidheamh linn deug. Chaidh 'A' Chreag', mar a chanas cuid ris an eilean, a thuineachadh san t-seachdamh linn deug le iasgairean Èireannach, Sasannach is Frangach a bha ag iasgach an truisg. B' e 'talamh an èisg' a bh' aig na h-Èireannaich air, oir b' e an t-iasg maoin nan daoine fad linntean. Chun an latha an-diugh, cluinnear a' bhuaidh mhòr a bh' aig na trì dùthchannan anns na fuinn agus ann an dòigh cluiche nan innealan-ciùil, anns na h-òrain agus anns an dualchainnt, agus chithear i anns an dannsa. Ach chan eil daoine cho eòlach air eachdraidh no dualchas nan Albannach a tha dìreach air aon sa cheud de shluagh an Talaimh Ùir.

B' e Srath Codroy air an taobh siar ceann-uidhe deireannach de bhuidheann dlùth de dh'eilthirich na Gàidhlig. Cha b' ann airson buannachd an iasgaich a thàinig iadsan ach airson pìos fearainn air an dèanadh iad am beòshlaint. Chan eil eachdraidh oifigeil an ama a' toirt mòran fiosrachaidh idir mun deidhinn no mu na thachair riutha, ach chùm iad beò an eachdraidh, an cultar agus dualchas na Gàidhlig fad ghinealaichean. Dh'fhaodadh gun cluinn thu fhathast corra abairt sa chòmhradh o latha gu latha. Tha a' chiall cheart (a' tadhal air taigh)

2

You may even catch the occasional turn of phrase in everyday conversation. The *cèilidh* still has its true meaning (literally, a house-visit) just as it did a hundred and fifty years ago, and a cup of tea is still an essential part of it, although the language now spoken in the kitchen is different.

All the songs, stories and tunes in this album originate in the kitchen of a first-generation Newfoundlander, Allan MacArthur. He was born in 1884, raised in the old homestead, and grew up to be the *seanchaidh* of his generation, as his mother had been before him. When he died, he left behind a priceless legacy of tradition, celebrated here by his children, grandchildren and great-grandchildren. Intensely proud of their Gaelic roots, they weave new songs and music into the old style as they keep alive the traditions of the *cèilidh*, or 'kitchen party' as some now say.

Allan MacArthur's grandparents were among the emigrants who sailed to 'America', as they called the entire continent in those days. His paternal grandfather was a MacArthur from the Inner Hebridean Isle of Canna, his maternal grandfather was a MacIsaac from Moidart and his grandmother a MacDonald from Glengarry. Like countless Highland emigrants, they left behind the hardship, poverty and post-Jacobite oppression that blighted the Gaels. They set sail with little but hope and faith, perhaps materially impoverished, yet in possession of one of the richest stores of oral tradition in the world.

When they eventually received land-grants in 'the Garden of Newfoundland' they were thankful to accept the challenge of carving out a living, clearing land for farming, and adapting to a new climate, landscape and neighbours speaking French, English or Mi'kmaq. At the same time, they retained the old Gaelic ways, particularly those connected

3

fhathast aig *cèilidh* dìreach mar a bh' aige o chionn ceud gu leth bliadhna, agus tha cupa tì fhathast cudromach, a dh'aindeoin 's nach eil an cànan fhathast sa chidsin.

Buinidh gach òran, sgeulachd is fonn air a' chlàr seo dhan chidsin aig Ailean MacArtair, fear dhen chiad ghinealach san Talamh Ùr. Rugadh e ann an 1884. Thogadh e san t-seann dachaigh agus dh'fhàs e suas gu bhith na sheanchaidh na ghinealach fhèin, mar a bha a mhàthair roimhe. Nuair a chaochail e, dh'fhàg e dìleab phrìseil de dhualchas. Tha sin air a chomharrachadh an seo leis a' chloinn, na h-oghaichean agus na h-iar-oghaichean aige. Tha iad air leth moiteil à dualchas na Gàidhlig. Bidh iad a' dèanamh òrain is ceòl ùr san t-seann stoidhle agus a' cumail beò dualchas a' chèilidh, no partaidh a' chidsin mar a chanas cuid an-diugh.

Bha seanair is seanmhair Ailein MhicArtair air cuid dhe na h-eilthirich a sheòl a dh'Ameireaga, mar a bh' aca air a' mhòr-thìr gu lèir aig an àm. Bha a sheanair air taobh athar na MhacArtair à Eilean Chanaigh agus b' e MacÌosaig à Mùideart a bha na sheanair air taobh a mhàthar agus bhuineadh a sheanmhair do Dhòmhnallaich Ghleanna Garadh. Cleas iomadh eilthireach Gàidhealach, chuir iad an cùl ris a' chruadal, ris a' bhochdainn agus ris an fhòirneart a thàinig air na Gàidheil an dèidh àm nan Seumasach. Nuair a sheòl iad, cha robh mòran aca ach dòchas is creideamh. Ged as dòcha nach robh mòran aca de stòras an t-saoghail, bha beul-aithris aca cho beartach 's a bh' air an t-saoghal.

Nuair a fhuair iad mu dheireadh taic-fearainn ann an 'Lios an Talaimh Ùir', bha iad taingeil gabhail ri gach duilgheadas a bha an lùib dòigh-beatha a dhèanamh dhaibh fhèin, talamh a ghlanadh airson àiteach agus fàs cleachdte ri gnàth-shìde is cumadh-tìre ùr agus nàbaidhean a bha a' bruidhinn Fraingis, Beurla no Mi'kmaq. Aig an aon àm, ghlèidh iad na

to language and culture. Every aspect of life had songs connected to it, from their daily tasks such as milking, churning and spinning to the gentle lulling of the baby to sleep each night. When daylight faded, their evening entertainment was the *taigh-cèilidh* (house visit) where neighbours would gather and nobody noticed the hours pass. Beside the kitchen stove, usually knitting or plying some craft, they could travel the world, listen to adventures of soldiers, sailors, pirates and smugglers, or stories about ghosts, fairies and witches. They could reminisce, recite genealogy, tell of local characters, the witty and the wise, the foolish and the strong. Sometimes the whole evening would be devoted to songs, music and step-dancing, depending on the company and the general atmosphere of the visit.

This was the world into which Allan MacArthur was born and in which he grew up, absorbing every available aspect of Gaelic tradition. He had a phenomenal memory, which he attributed simply to 'the schooling I got from God,' adding respectfully, 'and anything my mother told me, I never forgot.' Anyone privileged to have listened to him as he spoke of historical events in the Highlands, told his stories, sang Gaelic songs or quoted poetry can be thankful to have been in his presence.

In 1952, when the Celtic scholar, the late Professor Kenneth H. Jackson of Edinburgh University, described attributes of the ancient Gaelic bards of Scotland, his words could equally have applied to an outstanding

seann dòighean Gàidhealach, gu h-àraidh na nithean a bha co-cheangailte ri cànan is cultar. Bha òrain ceangailte ri gach nì nam beatha, eadar obair an latha mar bleoghan, maistreadh, snìomh agus tàladh an leanaibh air an oidhche. Nuair a thigeadh an oidhche, b' e an taigh-cèilidh an cur-seachad a bh' aca. Chruinnicheadh na nàbaidhean an sin agus cha bhiodh iad mothachail air an uair a' dol seachad. Ri taobh an stòbh sa chidsin, a' fighe no ri ceàird eile, shiubhaileadh iad an saoghal, ag èisteachd ri na thachair ri saighdearan, ri seòladairean, ri spùinneadairean-mara is ri cùl-mhùtairean, no ri sgeulachdan mu thaibhsean, sìthichean is bana-bhuidsichean. Bhruidhneadh iad mu na làithean a bh' ann, bhiodh iad ri sloinntearachd, agus dh'innseadh iad mu dhaoine às an àite – feadhainn a bha eirmseach is feadhainn a bha glic, feadhainn a bha gòrach is feadhainn a bha làidir. Uaireannan, chuireadh iad seachad am feasgar gu lèir ri òrain, ceòl agus dannsa-ceum, a rèir 's cò bha an làthair agus ciamar a bha daoine a' faireachdainn.

Seo an saoghal san do rugadh Ailean MacArtair agus anns an do dh'fhàs e suas, a' sùghadh a-steach gach nì co-cheangailte ri dualchas na Gàidhlig. Bha cuimhne aige a bha iongantach. Thuirt e fhèin gur ann air sgàth 'the schooling I got from God,' agus le urram, 'and anything my mother told me, I never forgot.' Duine sam bith a chuala e a' bruidhinn mu eachdraidh na Gàidhealtachd, ag innse sgeulachdan, a' gabhail òrain Ghàidhlig no ag aithris bàrdachd, faodaidh e a bhith gu math taingeil gun robh e na làthair.

Ann an 1952, nuair a rinn an sgoilear Ceilteach, an t-Ollamh Kenneth H. Jackson à Oilthigh Dhùn Èideann, iomradh air comharran seann bhàird na h-Alba, dh'fhaodadh e a bhith a' bruidhinn air Ailean MacArtair a bha cho sònraichte a thaobh dualchas na Gàidhlig:

tradition-bearer such as Allan MacArthur:

> In general, they were men of high intelligence and keen minds, passionately interested in tales, widely educated in the oral learning of the Gaelic race ... Their minds were not cluttered with all the miscellaneous rubbish with which we burden ours, and they were not in the habit of pigeon-holing knowledge in the form of written notes and forgetting it till it is wanted again, as we are.

By the late 1960s when I first met Allan MacArthur, he had long been regarded as the most knowledgeable Gaelic speaker and cultural custodian in the Valley. He was in no doubt that, whatever he knew about his culture, he had learned it the same manner as his parents and grandparents before him.

In 1913 Allan married Cecilia MacNeill, with whom he had four children—Lewis, Jim, Frank and Loretta. At the age of 24, sadly his young wife died after the birth of their baby daughter. Allan's mother was a godsend in helping to look after the children, till in 1923, he married Mary MacDonald. Frank reflected: "We were so lucky, you know," for she was the kindest, gentlest woman you could meet. Allan and Mary had seven children—John, Martin, George, Margaret, Dan, Sears and Gordon—and raised all eleven children in an entirely Gaelic-speaking household. [CD 2, track 10] Naturally, prayers and daily devotions were in Gaelic and the children were also nurtured with song, music, dancing and all the traditions of their people.

The local priests could all speak Gaelic, but, as in Scotland, it was the

San fharsaingeachd, b' e fir eanchainneil a bh' annta le inntinn gheur. Bha ùidh mhòr aca ann an sgeulachdan, agus bha ionnsachadh farsaing aca ann am beul-aithris luchd na Gàidhlig… Cha robh iad a' lìonadh an inntinn le sgudal mar a bhios sinne, agus cha robh e na chleachdadh aca a bhith a' sgaradh fiosrachadh agus a' cur tiotal air ann an notaichean sgrìobhte mar a bhios sinne, agus ga chur air dhìochuimhn' gus am bi feum againn air a-rithist.

Nuair a choinnich mi ri Ailean MacArtair deireadh nan 1960an, bha ainm aige mar an duine a b' eòlaiche sa Ghàidhlig agus mar fhear-gleidhidh an dualchais sa Ghleann. Cha robh teagamh sam bith aige, a thaobh càil sam bith a b' aithne dha mun chultar aige, nach do dh'ionnsaich e sin san aon dòigh ri a phàrantan agus a shinnsearan roimhe.

Ann an 1913 phòs Ailean Cecilia NicNèill agus bha ceathrar chloinne aca—Lewis, Jim, Frank agus Loretta. Nuair a bha i 24, chaochail a bhean nuair a rugadh an nighean aca. Bha màthair Ailein na tròcair dhan teaghlach a' coimhead às dèidh na cloinne gu 1923, nuair a phòs e Màiri Dhòmhnallach. Thuirt Frank, "We were so lucky, you know," oir bha i air tè cho coibhneil, gasta 's a bha riamh ann. Bha seachdnar chloinne aig Ailean is Màiri—John, Martin, George, Margaret, Dan, Sears agus Gordon—agus thogadh aona duine deug dhiubh ann an teaghlach nach robh a' bruidhinn ach Gàidhlig. [CD 2, trag 10] Gu nàdarra, bha iad ag ùrnaigh agus a' gabhail an Leabhair sa Ghàidhlig, agus thogadh a' chlann cuideachd le òrain, ceòl, dannsa is dualchas nan daoine.

Bha Gàidhlig aig gach sagart san sgìre, ach, dìreach mar a thachair ann an Alba, bha e na phoileasaidh aig Roinn Foghlaim an Talaimh Ùir

policy of the Newfoundland Education department to employ monoglot English-speaking teachers. Even after Confederation with Canada in 1949, the province was relatively late in providing schooling for all children. Though it was still common in the Sixties to meet Newfoundlanders who had never been to school, Allan and Mary (typical of the Scots) were, for their generation, well educated. Their own children followed the pattern, knew how to work hard, sing, dance, play music and, not least, to share the faith of their forebears.

The Clan MacArthur crest is *Fide et Opera*, and although I never heard Allan himself talk of it, the younger generations proudly claim it. Not only is it a connection with their MacArthur roots in Scotland, but it is also a reminder of the example set by the family that nurtured them— 'faith and work'.

Allan MacArthur liked nothing better than to be surrounded by those who shared his love of Gaelic song, music and oral tradition. When I visited with my parents to 'bring in the New Year' at the beginning of 1970, it was evident from the welcome we received that Allan was moved to have 'greetings from Scotland' at this time of year that all Scots hold dear. He and my mother, Peigi, compared how they brought in the New Year in days gone by. As I listened and tape-recorded, I heard (for the first time in my life) about a New Year custom that had died out in Skye before I was born, though my mother (b. 1919) was quite familiar

a bhith a' fastadh thidsearan aig nach robh ach Beurla. Fiù 's an dèidh Co-chaidreachas ri Canada ann an 1949, bha an roinn caran fadalach ann a bhith ag oideachadh na cloinne gu lèir. Ged a bha e fhathast bitheanta sna Seasgadan coinneachadh ri feadhainn on Talamh Ùr nach robh riamh san sgoil, bha Ailean agus Màiri (cleas muinntir Alba san fharsaingeachd) air an deagh oideachadh. Lean an clann an aon phàtran. Bha fios aca mar a dhèanadh iad obair chruaidh, ciamar a sheinneadh is a dhannsadh iad, ciamar a chluicheadh iad ceòl, agus rud eile a bha cudromach, ciamar a bhiodh pàirt aca ann an creideamh an sinnsearan.

'S e *Fide et Opera* suaicheantas Chlann MhicArtair, agus ged nach cuala mi riamh Ailean fhèin a' bruidhinn air, tha na ginealaich as òige glè mhoiteil às. Chan e a-mhàin gu bheil e gan ceangal rim freumhaichean ann an Alba, ach tha e cuideachd na chuimheachan dhaibh air an eisimpleir a thug an teaghlach aca dhaibh—'creideamh is obair'.

Cha robh càil a b' fheàrr le Ailean MacArtair na bhith air a chuartachadh le feadhainn a bha measail air òrain, ceòl is dualchas na Gàidhlig. Nuair a thadhail mi air còmhla ri mo phàrantan toiseach 1970 airson a' Bhliadhn' Ùr a thoirt a-steach, bha e follaiseach bhon fhàilte a fhuair sinn gun robh Ailean a' cur luach air 'dùrachd à Alba' aig àm dhen bhliadhna a tha cudromach do dh'Albannaich. Bha e fhèin agus mo mhàthair, Peigi, a' bruidhinn air mar a bhiodh iad a' toirt a-steach na Bliadhn' Ùire o chionn fhada. Fhad 's a bha mi ag èisteachd agus a' clàradh, chuala mi (airson a' chiad turas riamh) mu chleachdadh aig àm na Bliadhn' Ùire a bh' air a dhol à bith san Eilean Sgitheanach mus do rugadh mi, ged a bha mo mhàthair (r. 1919) gu math eòlach air na h-òige—Oidhche Challainn. (CD 2 Tragan 3 & 4) Nuair a dh'aithris Ailean an rann aigesan, bha e cho toilichte, agus chuir e iongnadh ormsa, nuair a dh'aithris Peigi a

with it from her youth—*Oidhche Challainn*. (CD 2 Tracks 3 & 4) When Allan recited his *rann* [rhyme] he was as delighted as I was amazed to hear Peigi recite *her* version from Skye. Everyone in the company was in their element to be part of a real, old-fashioned cèilidh, the likes of which we had never seen outside Gaelic Scotland—and even there, much of what we experienced had already faded. Naturally a few songs and tunes were part of it and Peigi contributed, as did my father, George, with his life-long love of playing the bagpipes. The teapot was refilled several times, and, it being New Year, there were the customary drams as you may hear from the recording—*Slàinte!* There were toasts too, and Allan's memorable remarks: " I don't think there's any country in the world that can put down Scotland for their poetry—I don't think so." When we were leaving their house to step into the snow, Allan told us, "Well, I would like to see you coming every week. I could keep you up all night telling you stories and singing you songs."

I mention this particular cèilidh, though we had many others, not so much because it marked a turning point in the year, but a turning point in my own life. Full force it struck me—still in my early twenties—how suddenly these old traditions can disappear if nobody passes them on. Sometimes circumstances outside our control can intervene. Two World Wars had managed to wipe out *Oidhche Challainn* in Skye because 'nobody had the heart to visit' when so many mourned the loss of husbands, fathers and sons. My own family is a case in point: there were four brothers at the start of the First World War, strapping young men, and only one, my grandfather, was left at the end of it.

Other times, however, there seems to be a mass oblivion of the

dreach fhèin às an Eilean Sgitheanach. Bha gach duine sa chuideachd cho sona oir bha iad a' gabhail pàirt ann an cèilidh ceart, dualchasach nach fhacas a leithid taobh a-muigh Gàidhealtachd na h-Alba. Agus fiù 's an sin fhèin, bha mòran dhe na dh'fhiosraich sinn air crìonadh. Gu nàdarrach, bha cuid dhe na h-òrain is dhe na puirt nam pàirt dheth, agus chuir Peigi riutha, mar a rinn m' athair, Seòras, a bha riamh cho measail air cluich na pìoba. Chaidh a' phoit-tì a lìonadh iomadh uair, agus, seach gur e a' Bhliadhn' Ùr a bh' ann, bha na dramaichean àbhaisteach a' dol, mar as dòcha a chluinneas tu sa chlàradh—*Slainte!* Bha deochan-slàinte ann cuideachd, agus cuid dhe na thuirt Ailean: " I don't think there's any country in the world that can put down Scotland for their poetry—I don't think so." Nuair a bha sinn a' fàgail an taighe aca agus a' dol a-mach dhan t-sneachd, thuirt Ailean: "Well, I would like to see you coming every week. I could keep you up all night telling you stories and singing you songs."

Tha mi ag ainmeachadh a' chèilidh seo gu h-àraidh, ged a bha iomadach fear eile againn, chan ann airson gun do chomharraich e tionndadh sa bhliadhna, ach airson 's gun do chomharraich e tionndadh na mo bheatha fhìn. Bha mi dìreach beagan is fichead ach bhuail e orm gu mòr mar a thèid dualchas à bith mura bi duine ga chumail a' dol. Uaireannan, tachraidh rudan air nach eil smachd againn. Chuir an dà Chogadh Mhòr às do dh'Oidhche Challainn san Eilean Sgitheanach oir cha robh duine ann an sunnd cèilidh nuair a bha uiread a' caoidh am fir, an athraichean agus am mic. Tha mo theaghlach fhìn na eisimpleir air an seo: bha ceathrar bhràithrean ann aig toiseach a' Chiad Chogaidh, òigearan tapaidh, agus cha robh ach aon fhear dhiubh beò aig deireadh a' chogaidh, agus b' e sin mo sheanair.

Uaireannan eile, saoilidh tu gu bheil an saoghal a' cur air

factors that rob us of our heritage, especially those with silvered screens. As Allan MacArthur said, just a few years after the coming of electricity, "When the television came in the front door, the stories went out the back." And, as everyone in the Valley knows, only strangers (English-speakers in Allan's time) knock on the front door, as family and friends use the back door beside the kitchen.

In that *cèilidh* Allan MacArthur demonstrated the importance of upholding the language, as it is the vehicle that carries tradition from one generation to the next. Gaelic had been the language of all my mother's family and she, like Allan and Mary's children, had no English when she went to school. It happened, however, that my generation had to speak English at home, as it was commonly thought children 'would get on better in life' if they learned English, and we learned no Gaelic at school. With my mother we learned plenty of Gaelic songs, and a few phrases, but New Year 1970 showed me that this is not enough to maintain a culture. Thus, I determined to learn to *speak* Gaelic so I might at least try to follow Allan MacArthur's example. I began my early recordings regretting that this could not be an all-Gaelic project because I was not fluent, then slowly realizing that it might have been for the best—had I spoken Gaelic in the first place, perhaps I might have taken it all for granted and therefore missed it completely. Over these four decades I can truly say that neither my interest in, nor enthusiasm for, the culture and tradition fade over time—if anything, along with my affection for the family, they increase, thanks to that New Year spent with Allan and Mary MacArthur.

That said, traditional folk culture cannot stand still if it is to remain alive. Subtle changes in an old song or tune are a sure sign of life, for, as

dhiochuimhn' nan rudan a tha a' toirt bhuainn ar dualchais, gu h-àraidh nithean co-cheangailte ri na filmichean milis. Mar a thuirt Ailean MacArtair, "When the television came in the front door, the stories went out the back." Agus, mar a tha fios aig a h-uile duine sa Ghleann, cha bhi ach coigrich (luchd na Beurla a thaobh Ailein) a' gnogadh air an doras-aghaidh.

Aig a' chèilidh sin, sheall Ailean MacArtair cho cudromach 's a tha e a bhith a' cumail suas a' chànain mar mhodh a tha a' toirt seachad dualchas bho aon ghinealach gu ginealach eile. B' i a' Ghàidhlig cànan teaghlach mo mhàthar agus, cleas clann Ailein is Màiri, cha robh Beurla aice nuair a chaidh i dhan sgoil. Ach, mar a thachair, bha aig a' ghinealach agamsa ri Beurla a bhruidhinn san dachaigh agus cha do dh'ionnsaich sinn Gàidhlig san sgoil. Dh'ionnsaich sinn iomadh òran Gàidhlig còmhla ri mo mhàthair, agus abairtean eile, ach sheall a' Bhliadhn' Ùr ann an 1970 dhomh nach eil sin gu leòr airson cultar a ghleidheadh. Mar sin, chuir mi romham gun ionnsaichinn a bhith a' *bruidhinn* na Gàidhlig airson agus gum bithinn co-dhiù a' leantainn eisimpleir Ailein MhicArtair. Nuair a thòisich mi a' clàradh an toiseach, bha aithreachas orm nach b' urrainn dhan phròiseact a bhith gu lèir sa Ghàidhlig seach nach robh mi fileanta. Mean air mhean, ge-tà, thuig mi gun robh e na b' fheàrr mar sin. Nan robh a' Ghàidhlig air a bhith agam aig an ìre sin, dh'fhaodadh nach bithinn air uiread de shùim a chur ann agus bhithinn air a chall gu tur. Feumaidh mi ràdh nach do lùghdaich m' ùidh no mo dhealas a thaobh a' chànain agus a thaobh an dualchais. Gu dearbh, ma thachair càil idir, 's e gun deach mo mheas am meud, dìreach mar a chaidh mo mheas air an teaghlach am meud, air sgàth na Bliadhn' Ùir' a chuir mi seachad còmhla ri Màiri is Ailean MacArtair.

Ach chan urrainn dualchas a bhith na thàmh ma tha e gu bhith beò.

long as someone is singing it, playing it, then it lives. Allan's older brother Murdoch, the song-maker of his generation, may have seen the writing on the wall when he began to turn his bardic talent to composing macaronic songs, mixing English lines with Gaelic. That way, everyone could join in or at least be amused. As often as not, however, only the Gael could catch the subtlety or punch line if there happened to be one.

There is no doubt that this ancient bardic strain, with its song-makers and poets, has continued through every generation right to the present day. Four generations of this remarkable family are represented here and although the language has now declined and been supplanted, it was not through choice: "That's how things were, and it happened so quickly." In his poem 'Forgotten Roots', Allan's grandson, Brendan MacArthur (Frank's son), reflected in 2007 on the language shift since he left high-school in 1968:

> "Ciamar a tha thu?"
> He asked me with a smile;
> 'Twas the first time I'd heard Gaelic
> In a very, very long time.
> "Glè mhath, glè mhath, chan eil mi gearan,"
> I respectfully replied.
> As he moved o'er the bench,
> Bid me sit by his side,
> "A bheil Gàidhlig agaibh?"
> His eyes twinkled in a gleam.
> "Tha mi ag ionnsachadh" was my sad reply…

Tha atharraichean beaga ann an seann òran no ann an seann fhonn na chomharra air beatha, oir, fhad 's a tha daoine ga sheinn no ga chluich, tha e fhathast beò. Dh'fhaodadh gun do thuig Murchadh, am bràthair bu shine aig Ailean, agus a bha na bhàrd, gun robh a' chrìoch air fàire nuair a thòisich e a' dèanamh òrain le loidhneachan ann an Gàidhlig is ann am Beurla. Mar sin, b' urrainn dhan a h-uile duine pàirt a ghabhail no a shaoilsinn èibhinn. Ach glè thric, b' e an Gàidheal a-mhàin a thuigeadh an teachdaireachd no an fhealla-dhà ma bha sin ann.

Mhair seann mhodh bàrdachd nam filidhean, le na bàird is na h-òranaichean, tro na ginealaich chun an latha an-diugh. Tha ceithir ginealaich dhen teaghlach iongantach seo a' nochdadh an seo, agus ged a chrìon an cànan agus a chaidh fear eile na àite, cha b' e gun do roghnaich iad sin: "That's how things were, and it happened so quickly." San dàn 'Forgotten Roots', tha ogha Ailein, Brendan MacArtair (mac Fhrangain), a' beachdachadh ann an 2007 mar a thàinig cànan eile am bàrr bho dh'fhàg e an àrd-sgoil ann an 1968:

> "Ciamar a tha thu?"
> He asked me with a smile;
> 'Twas the first time I'd heard Gaelic
> In a very, very long time.
> "Glè mhath, glè mhath, chan eil mi gearan,"
> I respectfully replied.
> As he moved o'er the bench,
> Bid me sit by his side,
> "A bheil Gàidhlig agaibh?"
> His eyes twinkled in a gleam.
> "Tha mi ag ionnsachadh" was my sad reply…

16

Translation: 'How are you?' … 'Very well, very well, I'm not complaining' … 'Do you speak Gaelic?' … 'I'm learning it' …]

Like his Uncle Murdoch before him, Brendan composes poems ranging across the spectrum—from amusing sit-com incidents to political, social and cultural issues, all grist to the satirist's mill. And, like Murdoch, he sometimes weaves both languages into his poetry, even though the balance has long-since tipped to the point where English predominates.

What has not changed over the generations, however, is the need to sing, compose, play music and dance—it is as strong today as ever. Allan and Mary would be proud of the achievements of their grandchildren and great-grandchildren, not only those represented here but others as well.

In the new songs composed in English by the younger generations, listeners could not fail to be struck by how Allan MacArthur features in several of them while his influence can be sensed through most of them. The track-notes give details but the songs and the music speak for themselves, as does this one, composed by Allan's grandson, Gordon:

> Looking on MacArthur's Island as many a time before
> Brings back so many memories of home,
> I remember Grandpa telling us of Scotland far away,
> And praying to God he'd make it there some day.

Allan MacArthur never did see his beloved Scotland, though he lived and died as one of the finest Gaelic tradition-bearers either side of the Atlantic— teacher, singer, historian, storyteller, rhymer, piper, fiddler, accordionist,

Cleas Mhurchaidh roimhe, bidh Brendan a' dèanamh iomadh seòrsa dàin—eadar feadhainn èibhinn is feadhainn air cùisean poilitigeach, sòisealta agus cultarach a tha measail aig a h-uile neach-aoir. Agus cleas Mhurchaidh, bidh e uaireannan a' fighe an dà chànan a-steach dhan bhàrdachd, fiù 's ged a tha làmh-an-uachdair aig a' Bheurla.

Ach tha aon rud nach do dh'atharraich thar nan ginealach, agus 's e sin an togradh gu bhith a' seinn, a' dèanamh òran, a' cluich ceòl agus a' dannsa. Tha sin cho làidir 's a bha e riamh. Bhiodh Ailean is Màiri gu math moiteil às na choilean an oghaichean agus an iar-oghaichean, chan e a-mhàin an fheadhainn a tha a' nochdadh an seo ach feadhainn eile cuideachd.

Chan urrainn dhan luchd-èisteachd gun a bhith a' mothachadh mar a tha Ailean MacArtair a' nochdadh ann am mòran dhe na h-òrain ùra Bheurla a tha an ginealach òg a' sgrìobhadh agus mar a dh'fhairichear buaidh Ailein sa mhòr-chuid dhiubh. Tha na notaichean a' toirt fiosrachadh mu na h-òrain agus tha an ceòl ga mhìneachadh fhèin, mar am fear seo, a rinn Gòrdan, ogha Ailein:

> Looking on MacArthur's Island as many a time before
> Brings back so many memories of home,
> I remember Grandpa telling us of Scotland far away,
> And praying to God he'd make it there some day.

Chan fhaca Ailean MacArtair Alba riamh, ged a bha e air fear cho cudromach 's a bh' ann air gach taobh dhen Chuan Siar a thaobh a bhith a' toirt seachad dualchas na Gàidhlig. Bha e na neach-teagaisg, na

dancer, craftsman, fireside philosopher and friend. Newfoundland can be proud of Allan MacArthur and of the legacy he left. As three generations of his family return to their roots for 'Homecoming Scotland 2009' it's time to recognize Newfoundland's Gaelic custodian, Allan MacArthur, whose passion for his language—*our* language—and culture is an example to us all.

Margaret Bennett
Ochtertyre, Scotland, 2009

sheinneadair, na eachdraiche, na sheanchaidh, na òranaiche, na phìobaire, na fhìdhlear, na chluicheadair air a' bhogsa, na dhannsair, na fhear-ceàird, na fheallsanaiche an tac an teine agus na charaid. Faodaidh An Talamh Ùr a bhith moiteil à Ailean MacArtair agus a dhìleab. Nuair a tha trì ginealaich dhe theaghlach a' tilleadh a dh'Alba airson 'Tilleadh Dhachaigh 2009', tha an t-àm ann aithne a thoirt do neach-gleidhidh na Gàidhlig san Talamh Ùr, Ailean MacArtair. Bu chòir dha dhealas dha chànan—ar cànan-ne—agus dhan dualchas, a bhith na eisimpleir dhuinn uile.

Mairead Bennett
Uachdar Thìre, Alba, 2009

Key to codes and abbreviations

- Album titles and details are given for all commercial recordings used with permission.
- **Comp.** = Names(s) of composer(s) of song or tune
- **Rec. MB** = Recorded by Margaret Bennett in year shown (folklore fieldwork, archived).
- **Ref. LS, pp.** # = Words and/or music published in *The Last Stronghold: The Scottish Gaelic Traditions of Newfoundland by Margaret* Bennett (Canongate Publishing, Edinburgh and Breakwater Books, St. John's), 1989. Page numbers are referenced.
- **Trad.** = Traditional (song, poem, tune, saying, toast).
- **Note:** The Gaelic Orthographic Conventions (2005) have been used throughout **except** when transcribing vocable syllables in songs where the sound of the syllable would alter by using the grave accent. For example, hó (**not** hò) and ré (**not** rè).

MacArthur's Cèilidh **Dìleab**
Ailein Cèilidh MhicArtair

1. A toast to Scotland Trad.
Allan MacArthur. Rec. MB, 1969.

Scotland, thy mountains
Thy valleys and fountains
The home of the poets
The birthplace of songs!

2. 'Illean Bithibh Sunndach (Lads, be happy) Trad.
Allan MacArthur, with sons George, Martin and John & Margaret Bennett. Rec. MB, 1969. Ref. LS, pp. 157-58.

According to Allan, 'this song was composed in Scotland. It was a crowd that left ..., crossing the Atlantic from *an t-Eilean Sgitheanach*, and coming out, you know, in America.'

CHORUS
[O]'illean bithibh sunndach a-null air a' bhòidse
Bhith fàgail ar dùthcha gun dùil ri tilleadh beò innt'
O 'illean bithibh sunndach a-null air a' bhòidse.

1. Mise tha fo ghruaman
    Dol a' shiubhal chuantan
    Air soitheach caol a' bhruaillein
    Gam fhuadach thar m' eòlais.

2. 'S mise tha fo mhì-thlachd
    On dh'fhàg mi 'n t-Eilean Sgitheanach
    'S thoir dùrachd mo chridhe-sa
    Dhan nighean dh'fhàg mi bhrònach.

23

3. 'Illean cridheil gaolach
   Togaibh rith' a h-aodach
   Chan fhaigh mi 'n tir mo ghaoil sibh
   Cho slaodte an àm seòladh.

4. 'Illean cridheil ceanalta
   Deanaibh riof a theannachadh
   Dar thig an stoirm an ath-bhliadhna
   Bu mhath leinn a bhith còmhla.

5. Gur mise tha fo èislein
   Ri còmhdhail na..
   On d'fhag mi thu eudail
   Air fèill an lnbhir Lòchaidh.

6. 'S ioma rud a chunna mi
   Tha cuir mòran mulaid orm
   An-diugh gun d' rinn iad tuilleadh dheth
   MacDougall bhith na chòcair.

7. Gur mis tha fo ghràin dheth
   Dar chi mi fear dubh, grànda
   'S ann theannas mi ri rànaich
   Nuair chi mi bàrr a mheòirean.

8. Dar ruigeas sinn Ameireaga
   Cha bhi dìth no deireas oirnn
   Gu faigh sinn pailteas coilleadh
   Ann an Eilean Nova Scotia.

You can leave an *t-Eilean Sgitheanach* today and be back home again tomorrow... but when my people came out, the MacIsaacs, it took them seven weeks on the boat from the time...*bhon deach iad air bàta ann an Tobar Mhoire, agus*...landed on the *Gut o' Canso. Nuair a chunnaic mo Sheanair 's mo Sheanamhair an t-àit, nam biodh long a' dol a dh'Alba air ais cha tigeadh iad air tìr, ach bha 'm bàta dol do dh'Astrailia.* They would never have landed if the boat was going back to Scotland.

TRANSLATION:
Chorus: Lads, be happy going over on the voyage/ Leaving our land without any hope of returning to it alive/ Lads be happy going over on the voyage.

1. I feel so gloomy/ Going to sail the seas/ In the slender, storm-tossed vessel/ Driven out of my homeland.
2. I am so downhearted/ Since leaving the Isle of Skye/ Take my heart-felt blessings/ To the girl I left grieving.
3. Happy, dear lads/ Put up her sails/ in my beloved land I will not find you/ So sluggish at the time of sailing.
4. Hearty, handsome lads/ Reef the sails tightly/ when the storm comes next year/ We would work well together.
5. I feel dejected/ Meeting the..[?]./ Since I left you, my dear one/ At the fair in Inverlochy.
6. I have seen many things/ that saddened me/ Today they have made it even worse/- Making MacDougall the galley cook.
7. I feel repelled/ When I see a swarthy, ugly man/ it's enough to make me cry/ To see his (dirty) fingernails.
8. When we get to America/ We will not have lack or need/ We'll find plenty of wood/ In the island of Nova Scotia.

You can leave the Isle of Skye today and be home again tomorrow...but when my people came out, the MacIsaacs, it took them seven weeks on the boat from the time they went on the boat in Tobermory [Isle of Mull] and landed on the *Gut o' Canso* [Cape Breton]. When my grandfather and grandmother saw the place, if the boat had been going back to Scotland, they wouldn't have landed; but the boat was going to Australia. They would have never have landed if the boat was going back to Scotland.

On another occasion Allan had the following as verse 4, which is very significant because his people actually had to get from Canna to Tobermory on the Isle of Mull and from there they set out across the Atlantic.

> 'Illean cridheil togarrach
> Òlaidh sibh na thogaras
> 'S e 's ann an Tobar Mhoire
> Ni sinn coinneamh ris a' chòmhlan

TRANSLATION: Hearty, happy fellows /Drink as much as you like / It will be in Tobermory /We shall meet up with the company.

It may seem curious that they should sail from Mull as, even today with modern ferries, this is a difficult journey—one look at the map is enough to deter tourists! Testifying to the strength of Gaelic oral tradition, however, the MacArthur family account is entirely accurate as it is confirmed by a parallel report from Angus MacDonald who was born in Canna in 1863. The recording was made in 1949 by the late Dr Calum MacLean and sent to me in 1988 by John Lorne Campbell of Canna who also translated it:

> Chuir Clann 'ic Nìll uabhas dhaoine as an eilean. Cha chreid mi nach d'fhalbh trì fichead teaghlaichean as a' seo ri linn m'athair a bhith 'na dhuine òg. 'S e a' rud bu mhiosa dheth, cha n-fhaigheadh iad fuireach as a' rìoghachd seo fhéin. Bha iad air son iad a dhol fairis co dhiù. 'S ann a Chanada a chuireadh iad. Chuala mi gun deach iad air bòrd an Tobar Mhoire

TRANSLATION:
The MacNeills [who owned Canna at that time] put a terrible number of people out of the island. I believe that sixty families left when my father was a young man. The worst of it was that they couldn't remain in this country. Anyway, they wanted them to go overseas. They were sent to Canada. I heard that they embarked at Tobermory.

3. **Gura Bòidheach am Bàta** (Bonnie is the ship) Trad.
Allan MacArthur. Rec. MB, 1970. Ref. LS, pp. 158-60.

After every verse you're supposed to sing the chorus, you know, so all hands would sing the rounds. Oh, you wouldn't hear yourself talking when they would be about fifteen or sixteen singing at one time!

CHORUS
Gura bòidheach am bàta
Bhith ga feitheamh aig sàile
Nuair a thèid na siùil bhàna
A chàradh ri cruinn.

1. Dar a thog sinn an t-acair
   'S a chaidh i fo astar
   Chan e gillean gun tapachd
   A smachdaicheadh i.

2. Nuair a thug sinn gu cuan i
   'S i air bhàrr nan tonn uaine
   'S i ga fàgail air fuaradh
   Gus na dh'fhuadaicheadh sinn

3. Chaidh i throimh na caoiltean
   'S i cho luath ris a' ghaothaidh
   'S chum na gillean rith' h-aodach
   Gus na (? sgaoil i fo? druim).

4. Labhair Eòghain mo bhràthair
   "Deanaibh riofadh gu làidir
   Saoil an dèan i ar bàthadh
   Fhad 's bhios sàile fo druim?"

5. A' dol timcheall air Seona
   Dh'fhàs an fhairge glè ghreannmhor
   Dh'iarr na gillean *reef-hank*
   A chur gu teann san t-seòl chinn.

6. Seachad beulaibh Dhùn Oraigh
   Chaidh a riofadh gu dòigheil
   'S e bhith 'g èisteachd a crònain
   Ceòl bu deònaiche leinn.

7. Nuair a chuir sinn gu *port* i
   'S a dh'fheuch sinn a cosnadh
   'S ó gu feumadh i doctair
   Fhuair i lot… cinn.

8. Dar a bha mi sa ghàbhadh
   Rinn mi smaointean neo dhà ann
   Mo leannan 's mo chàirdean
   Bhith ga fàgail gam chaoidh.

9. Nam biodh fhios aig mo mhàthair
   Dar a bha mi sa ghàbhadh
   Bhiodh i guidhe gu làidir
   Rìgh nan Gràs a bhith leinn.

10. Dar a ràine sinn Grianaig
    Taighean cusbainn gan clìoradh
    Uisge-beatha cha b' fhiach e
    Ach am fìon ga thoirt dhuinn.

11. Gheibh sinn canabhas ùr dhi
Agus rudan bhon bhùthaidh
Cruinn ghasta na giùthsaich
'S nach lùb gun droch shìd'.

TRANSLATION:
Chorus: Beautiful is the ship, as we await her at sea/ When the white sails are set on her masts.
1. When we weighed anchor and she gathered speed / The lads to handle her would need to be sturdy.
2. When we took her to sea, cresting the green waves/ She was held to windward until we were under way
3. She sailed through the narrows/ Swift as the wind /The boys kept adding sail until she [?had plenty] water under her keel.
4. My brother, Ewen, said 'Reef the sails tightly! / I wonder if she'll drown us/while there is sea-water under her keel?'
5. Going round Shona the sea became very rough / The boys asked for a reef-hank/To be tightened in the head-sail.
6. Passing by Dun Oraigh/she was well reefed / Listening to her humming along/ was the music we like best.
7. When we turned her to port and tried to get her under control / [I thought] she would need a 'doctor' for she got a gash in her head.
8. When I was in the danger/ I had thought or two of/My sweetheart and my friends/ who would be left mourning me.
9. If my mother had known/ when I was in peril / She would have earnestly prayed/ God of Grace to be with us.
10. When we reached Greenock, / clearing customs /Whisky wasn't good enough/ it was wine they gave us.
11. We shall get her new canvas /and things from the shop / Fine masts of fir, /That won't bend without bad weather.

NOTE re. verse 10: Greenock would have been the first port of call of the ship, taking on more passengers before crossing the Atlantic. Even for 21st century shipping, Hebridean seas can be fearsomely rough, and in stormy weather it is quite common for ferries to be cancelled.

4. Them songs came from Scotland
Allan MacArthur. Rec. MB, 1970. Ref. LS, pp. 146.

> Them songs came from Scotland. They were composed in Scotland, my grandmother, you know, she was full of songs and my mother learned her songs. And my mother knowed sixty songs, and some they'd be double [8-line] verses. She couldn't sing English songs, only all Gaelic—war songs and everything else.

5. Ailean Duinn (Brown-Haired Allan) Trad.
Allan MacArthur. Rec. MB, 1970. Ref. LS, pp. 165-66.

This song dates to the Napoleonic Wars, still a topic of current conversation when Allan's grandparents left Scotland. Gaelic scholar Dr John MacInnes (who met three of Allan's family when they visited Scotland) suggests that it may be from the Egyptian campaign of 1798.

> CHORUS:
> Hù a hù Ailein Duinn
> Ailein Duinn bhòidhich
> 'S a hù a hù Ailein Duinn.
>
> 1. Ailein Duinn a' chùl dualaich
>   Bhuidhe chuachagaich bhòidhich
>
> 2. Ailein Duinn a' chùl bhuidhe
>   Bhith gad chumha 's tu brònach
>
> 3. 'S truagh nach robh mi san fhiabhras
>   Man d' fhuair mi riamh beò thu.

Chorus: Hoo-a-hoo, brown-haired Allan (Allan Donn)/ Handsome Allan Donn/ S-ah-hoo-a-hoo Allan Donn.
1. Allan Donn with the lovely hair/ in beautiful golden curls.
2. Allan Donn with your blond hair/ I'm lamenting you in your sorrow.
3. Pity I wasn't sick with fever/ Before l ever met you in life.

6. Tom Dey & Calum Crùbach set Trad.
Johnnie Archie MacDonald (Fiddle). Rec. MB, 1970.

The first tune is a variant on one by Scottish composer J Scott Skinner (1843 – 1927), and the second a favourite *port-à-beul, Calum Crùbach.*

7. Fear a' Bhàta (The Boat Man) Trad.
Frank MacArthur. Rec. MB, 1990.

This song is well-known in Scotland (and Ireland) though it is generally sung to a slower tempo than in Newfoundland where the pace suits the milling. (Allan had a longer version as 'the boys' usually relied on him to carry the verses while they all joined in.)

> CHORUS:
> Fear a' bhàta 's na ho-ro-èile
> Fear a' bhàta 's na ho-ro-èile
> Fear a' bhàta 's na ho-ro-èile
> Gun dar a slàinte is càit' an tèid thu.
>
> [Mo shoraidh slàn leat 's gach àit an tèid thu]

1. 'S tric mo shùilean air chnoc as àirde
   Feuch a' faic mi fear a' bhàta
   An tig thu nochd no 'n tig thu màireach
   'S mur tig thu idir 's gur truagh a tha mi.

2. Fear a' bhàta 's na ho-ro-èile (etc)

TRANSLATION:
Chorus: The boatman, sna-ho-ro-ayluh/ x3/ Here's a health to you wherever you go.
1. Often I look from a high hill/ To see if I can see the boat man/ Will you come back tonight or even tomorrow/ If you don't arrive at all, how sad I'll be.

8. Tha Mi Sgìth (I am Tired) Trad.
Allan MacArthur. Rec. MB, 1970. Ref. LS, pp. 169.

Sometimes known as *Buain a' rainich*, this old song also goes well on the bagpipes. In Scotland it is sung or played at a much slower tempo than Allan's step-dance variant.

1. Tha mi sgìth 's mi leam fhìn
   Buain a' rainich buain a' rainich
   Tha mi sgìth 's mi leam fhìn
   H-uile là 'm ònar.

2. Cùl an tomain, bràigh an tomain
   Cùl an tomain bhòidhich
   Cùl an tomain, bràigh an tomain
   H-uile latha 'm ònar.

TRANSLATION:
1. I am tired and alone/ Cutting bracken, cutting bracken/ I am tired and alone/Every day

on my own.

2. At the back of the hillock, at the top of the hillock/ At the back of the beautiful hillock / At the top of the hillock, at the top of the hillock/ Every day on my own.

9. Kitchener's Army. Comp. Piper-Major G.S. MacLennan
Leonard (fiddle) & Sears MacArthur (guitar). Rec. MB, 1990.

This 2/4 pipe march is almost as well-known as the famous World War I recruitment poster of Kitchener himself—'Your country needs you!' The steady tempo and pace of Leonard's playing backed by Sears would inspire anyone to march.

10. Ged Tha Mi Gun Chrodh, Gun Aighean
(Though I Have No Cattle or Heifers) Trad.
Frank MacArthur. Rec. MB, 1990. Ref. LS, pp. 171.

This old traditional song appears in many Gaelic song collections in Scotland. Frank recalled this verse and chorus from his father's singing at the millings.

> CHORUS:
> Ged tha mi gun chrodh, gun aighean,
> Gun chrodh laoigh, gun chaoraich agam;
> Ged tha mi gun chrodh, gun aighean,
> Gheibh mi fhathast òigear grinn.

> 1. Ged tha mi gun chrodh, gun chaoraich,
> Chan eil mi gun bhòidheach aodainn.
> Dhèanainn breacan a bhiodh saor dhuit,
> Agus aodach a bhiodh grinn.

Chorus: Though I have no cattle or heifers/ No cows in calf, or sheep/ Though I have no cattle or heifers/ I shall yet find a fine young man.
1. Though I have no cattle or sheep/ I have a bonny face/ I would make a plaid that would cost you little/ And some fine clothes.

11. Gathering to sing
Frank MacArthur. Rec. MB, 1980, and Kenneth Goldstein.

Frank describes what it was like, even after they stopped spinning and weaving cloth they would still get together in someone's house to sing.

12. A Mhairi Dhubh a hù a ho (Dark Haired Mary) Trad.
Allan MacArthur, with sons George, Martin, John and Margaret Bennett. Rec. MB, 1970. Ref. LS, pp. 62-63.

No sooner had Allan begun this old favourite than everyone round the table grabbed the cloth to mill it. Though the 'thump' of a cotton tablecloth may not have quite the same resonance as the more dense sound of homespun wool, yet the song, the atmosphere and the enjoyment are totally authentic. And when the song ends, George expresses his joy of the moment with "*Suas e! Suas, a bhodaich!*" Everyone understands the idiom and laughs—they all know that Allan got the 'drive' just right!

Once in a while (and perhaps in honour of 'Uncle George') the phrase can still be heard in the Valley though most folk speak only English. It's usually called out to the musicians to encourage them to step up the tempo of the music, though it literally translates "Up with it! Up with it, old man!" Elsewhere in Newfoundland it could be "Heave it outa ya, ol' man!"

CHORUS:
A Mhàiri Dhubh na hù o hó
A Mhàiri Dhubh o rio ró
A Mhàiri Dhubh na hù o hó
Tha m' inntinn trom bhon dhealaich mi
Ri Màiri Dhubh o hù o hó.

1. Latha dhomh 's mi dol air sràid
   Cò thachair orm ach mo ghràdh
   O gu dearbh cha tog thu làmh
   Cha bhi mi slàn mur faigh mi thu.

2. 'S ann ort fhèin a dh'fhàs a' ghruag
   Figheachanan sìos mud chluais
   Ribinnean ga chumail suas
   Is prìne cinn ga theannachadh.

3. Fhad 's a chì mo shùil a' ghrian
   Tighinn bhon ear 's a' dol an iar
   Air fear liath cha bhi mo mhiann
   'S na ciabhagan a' tanachadh.

4. Mhàiri lurach anns a' ghleann
   Aig a bheil a' mhala chaol
   'S ann a mach Àirigh nan Caol
   A thug mi 'n gaol nach b' aithreach leam.

5. 'S truagh nach mise 's tu fhéin
   Bha sa ghleann far 'm biodh na fèidh
   'S binn' thu na 'n fhidheall air ghleus
   'S am beus an déidh a theannachadh.

6. 'S truagh nach mise bha fon fhòid
   Ann an ciste chaol nam bòrd
   Man tug mi mo ghaol cho mòr
   A sheòladair na mharaiche.

TRANSLATION:
Chorus: My black-haired Mary na-hu-o-ho/ (x3)/ My mind is heavy since we parted.
1. One day out walking/ Who should I meet but my love/ O surely you haven't given your hand/ For I can't thrive without you.
2. What beautiful hair you have/ Plaits down round your ears/ Tied up with ribbons/ And neatly pinned in place.
3. So long as I can see the sun/ Rising in the east and setting in the west/ A grey-haired man I would not wish for/ with his thinning locks.
4. Lovely Mary in the glen/ With the slender [eye]brow(s)/ It was out on Airigh nan Caol/ I gave the love I have not regretted.
5. It's a pity that you and I were not/ In the glen where the deer are/ Your voice sweeter than a well-tuned fiddle/ With the base string tightened.
6. I wish I had been under the sod/ In a narrow wooden coffin/ Before I gave such great love/ To a sailor or a seaman.

13. Òran an Tombaca (The Tobacco Song) Comp. Murdoch MacArthur

Allan MacArthur, sons George, Martin, John & M. Bennett. Rec. MB, 1970, and Herbert Halpert. Ref. LS, pp. 173-74.

At the end of the milling, when their cloth is thick enough, the final two songs, each with a special function, are sung, as Allan explains:

Now when the cloth'd be all fixed up, then they'd get a piece of board about six inches wide and probably four feet long and they would roll it up. Now I don't know what they call it in English,

you know, what we used to call it when the cloth was rolled up—
ga chur an coinneal. This is a song we generally use when we'd be
through milling the cloth, we'd roll it up, and we would be slapping
the cloth. It's rolled up, and stretched out and rolled up, and we
used the song to slap it right down ... For that everybody would
be slapping like this, their hands slapping the cloth, you know,
beating it down, taking the wrinkles out of it. You'd have a spell
on this side and then you'd turn it over and you'd do the other
side. Well then, you'd do that twice, then it was okay. There's a
separate song for that—it goes faster. And then you'd put it out in
the sun to dry, you see, the next day, and then it was fit for the old
people to cut out clothes, whether it was a coat or a vest or pants.

CHORUS:
Fal fal fal de re ro
Fal fal fal de rà
Fal e ré o fal de re o
Fal de re ro re ro rà.

1. 'S binne leam na gogail coilich
   Moch a ghoireadh anns an tom
   Torghan de bhotal ri glainne
   Agus duine thogas fonn.

2. Gur e bhuaidh a th' air an ruma
   Bheir e air duine bhith luath
   Bidh fear a' dannsa le chasan
   Bidh fear san leabaidh na shuain.

37

3. Gur e mo ghaol an tombaca
   'S mòr an tlachd a ghabhainn dhìot
   'S tric a chuir mi unnad tasdan
   Cha do chreach thu duine riamh.

4. H-uile fear nach bi rud aige
   Gur math leis gun tighinn nam chòir
   Nuair chì e mise ga chagnadh
   Cuiridh car tarsainn na shròin.

5. 'S iomadh mìle chuir mi riamh dhìom
   Cumail na fiacail air dòigh
   Ach chan fhaighinn iad ro dheiseil
   Dar nach biodh esan nan còir.

6. Fàsaidh mi mar loman chosach
   Fàsaidh mi nam chrogan ruadh
   Fàgaidh modh mi agus maise
   Caillidh mi claisneachd mo chluas.

7. Falbhaidh mi sin dha na bùithean
   Far am bi mo rùn air làmh
   Gu faighinn cairteal o Phenny
   Ged nach biodh teachd a'm an còrr.

TRANSLATION:
Chorus: Fal fal fal de re ro/ Fal fal fal de rà/ Fal e ré o fal de re o/ Fal de re ro re ro rà.
1. Sweeter to me than the clucking of a moorcock/ as it crows early on the hillock/ is the clink of bottle on glass/ and a man who will sing a song.
2. Tobacco, you are my love/ you give me great pleasure/ Many a shilling I've spent on

you / but you've never ruined anyone.

3. The effect of rum/ Makes one man go faster/ it sets another man's feet dancing,/ and some lie in bed fast asleep.
4. The one who has none/ would prefer not to come near me/ when he sees me chewing/ He turns up his nose.
5. Many a mile I've travelled/ to keep my teeth satisfied/ But I wouldn't find them so ready/ without tobacco to keep them going.
6. I'll become like some useless bald man/ I'll become like an earthen crock/ My manners and beauty will leave me/ I'll lose my hearing.
7. I'll go to the shops then/where my love [tobacco] is at hand/ I'll get a quarter (ounce) from Penny/ though I couldn't afford any more.

14. O Cò Bheirinn Leam? (Oh, Who would I Take with Me?) Trad. Allan MacArthur. Rec. MB, 1970. Ref. LS, pp. 176-77.

The milling concludes with a song for "slapping the cloth down to take the wrinkles out"— *òran basaidh*, as the Gaels call such songs. Versions of this one turn up in Gaelic Scotland, where, as in Newfoundland, one would be very unlikely to hear the same text sung twice, even by the same the singer, as verses are usually improvised on each occasion. The idea is to tease the company by playfully bringing individual names into verses of the songs, to make them laugh, blush, or react. It is probably no coincidence that the 'little boy' in Allan's first verse went by the name of 'Young'—just before he began singing, his life-long friends, Mr & Mrs Young, dropped in for a visit. The irony is that only Mrs Young (née MacIsaac) had Gaelic, whereas her husband was from a French family.

> CHORUS:
> 'S o cò bheirinn leam
> Air an luing Èireannaich?
> O cò bheirinn leam?

1. 'N gille beag aig Seonaidh Young
   Air an luing Èireannaich

2. Dhìreadh tu barra nan crann
   Air an luing Èireannaich

3. Thèid e fodha 's ni e plumb
   Air a' ghrunnd èiridh e.

TRANSLATION:
Chorus: Oh, who would I take with me/ On the Irish ship/Oh, who would I take with me?
1. Johnny Young's little boy / On the Irish ship
2. You would climb to the top of the mast/ On the Irish ship
3. He'll go under with a plonk! / and rise up from the deep.

15. A Chailin Dhuinn Bhon Dh'fhàg Thu Mi (Brown-Haired Maiden …) Trad.
Frank MacArthur. Rec. MB, 1990. Ref. LS, pp. 172.

This is one of several macaronic songs from the Valley where using two languages (sometimes French and English) can allow everyone to join in a chorus (Allan had two additional Gaelic verses of this song; LS, pp. 173).

> CHORUS:
> A chailin dhuinn bhon dh'fhàg thu mi
> Not at all in fun with you
> Chaidh mi chall nam preas an dé
> And that's the way we used to be

1. You were bonnie, you were bright
    You were handsome and polite
    And though you were so very nice
    I don't intend to marry you.

2. If I had wings like a dove
    I would fly the airs above
    I would go to see my love
    Who left me dull this evening.

3. Many a one that I had run
    Since the first that I begun
    I will try the best I can
    To rig a plan of leaving you.

4. When I saw you in the boat
    It made my heart so sick and sore
    When I saw you on the shore
    My heart was more to grieve with you

5. Many a night that I came home
    Sitting down a while alone
    Looking over at our home
    And thinking of my dearest one.

TRANSLATION:
Chorus: [My] brown-haired maiden, when you left me/… I got lost [?in the woods?] yesterday…

16. King George IV (strathspey), **Muileann Dubh** (reel) Trad.
Leonard & Sears MacArthur. Rec. MB, 1990.

The strathspey rhythm, a great favourite with step-dancers, is one of the distinguishing features of Canada's Scottish music. It sets the Valley apart from the rest of Newfoundland, where jigs and reels are more common.

17. Dominion Mine Strike Song Trad.
Frank MacArthur with family. Rec. MB, 1990. Ref. LS, pp. 183-85.

As a youngster Frank heard his father talk of the time he worked in a Cape Breton coal mine, though life underground was definitely not for Allan. Back home in the Valley, however, *The Dominion Mine Strike Song* became part of his repertoire. When I first heard him sing it, he detected my recognition of the tune. "It's the same as *Gur gile no leannan na 'n eal' air an t-snàmh* by Ewan MacLachlan," he explained. Then he launched into a few verses of it interspersed with the bard's singable translation, 'Not a swan on the lake or the foam on the shore'. And just in case the company still didn't appreciate the true greatness of the Scottish Gaelic bards, Allan took the opportunity to enlighten us: that same Lochaber man translated Homer's Iliad from Greek into Gaelic! (Allan's text Ref. LS, pp. 184). Returning to *The Dominion Mine Strike Song*, as the 1990 recording was of better quality than the one made in 1970, here's Frank to sing the song:

> CHORUS:
> Air fàillirinn, ìllirinn, ùillirinn, ò,
> Air fàillirinn, ìllirinn, ùillirinn, ò,
> Air fàillirinn, ìllirinn, ùillirinn, ò,
> There's policemen and soldiers wherever you go.

1. Come all you young fellows who knew friends of mine
   You'll always remember the year nineteen-nine
   A dirtier crowd you could never find
   And those who were scabbing were down in the mine.

2. The strike it began in the morning so dark,
   To see those poor fellows would break a man's heart,
   Parading the streets in their badges so bright
   And mind you those fellows they think they're all right.

3. That day at Dominion the strike it did start,
   The Mayor and the Council they thought they were smart,
   They called on the soldiers with cannons and lead
   And doctors and nurses looked after the dead.

4. There's a cop from Loch Lomond who walks a big track
   And if you go near him he'll leap on your back,
   There's old Martin Healey and Johnny MacLeod
   And to see those poor fellows would make a man proud.

5. There's Mr George Dunfy, I nearly forgot,
   He's neither an official, nor is he a cop,
   But from living a hard life and suffering from piles
   He's now just as thin as a three-cornered file!

6. Success to John Luscombe, I wish him good luck,
   He's the only town father that had any pluck
   When the Mayor and the Council they sought us to kill,
   Well, he fought and he fought and he'll fight for us still.

18. This Loch Lomond Here
Frank MacArthur. Rec. MB, 1990.

And, just to be sure there's no confusion about the origin of the 'cop from Loch Lomond', Frank (like his father) offered these details by way of explanation.

19. Trip to Mabou Ridge & High Road to Linton Trad.
Sear MacArthur (Accordion). Rec. MB, 1990.

To folk in the Valley, directions to Loch Lomond are better followed via local landmarks, such as the Campbell's house—many a good *cèilidh* there. When Allan's son, Sears, married Marie, they made their home with Mrs Campbell, who was widowed by then. She was as welcoming as any and loved to sit rocking a grandchild to sleep to the sound of the music. The walls could resonate with Sears on accordion but the music never seemed to disturb the baby!

20. Òl an Deoch air Làmh mo Rùin (Drink to health of my love) Trad.
Allan MacArthur and sons George, Martin and John. Rec. MB, 1970. Ref. LS, pp. 164-65.

Whatever the occasion (and often for no particular occasion) there is always an opportunity to raise a glass 'for good health'. And between times, the song can be used at the milling boards:

CHORUS
Òl an deoch air làmh mo ruin
Deoch slàint' air fear an tùir
Òl an deoch air làmh mo ruin

1. 'S mi a' leigeil às na seisreach
   Tha 'm feasgar a' leagadh driùchd.

2. Òladh ga' nach òladh càch i
   Biodh mo phàirt aig ceann a' bhùird.

TRANSLATION:
Chorus: Drink to the health of my love/ Here's health to the man of the tower/ Drink to the health of my love.
1. As I loose the plough team/ The evening is shedding dew.
2. Whether or not others will drink/ My portion will be at the head of the table.

21. A toast to whisky!
Allan MacArthur. Rec. MB, 1969. Ref. LS, pp. 73.

When I'm dead and in my grave
For no more whisky I will crave
But on my tomb those letters wrote:
'Many's the glass went down my throat!'

22. Bha Mi'n raoir ag Òl
(Last Night I Was Drinking) Trad.
Martin MacArthur. Rec. MB, 2006.

'Another of my father's,' Martin laughed when this little song came up at a cèilidh with his sister Margaret and her husband Leo. What delighted me even more than the song was the fact that you could still hear Gaelic in the Codroy Valley in the twenty-first century, and from a Newfoundland-born speaker at that.

> Bha mi' n raoir ag òl,
> Tha mi' n diugh gu tinn,
> 'S iomadh *cent* a choisinn mi 's a chuir mi ann
> Feumas mi an-drast' bhith sguir an dram.

TRANSLATION:
Last night I was on the drink/ Today I'm feeling ill/ Every cent I earn goes on drink/ I'll now have to put a stop to the drams.

23. Ho Rò Mo Nighean Donn Bhòidheach Trad.
Frank MacArthur and family chorus. Rec. MB, 1990. Ref. LS, pp. 160-61.

Wherever the Scottish Gaels settled, at home or abroad, this song followed them. In Scotland, however, Edinburgh Professor Stuart Blackie's standardized printed version of the song supplanted local variants. School children all over Scotland were taught Blackie's popular English version, "Ho ro my Nut-Brown Maiden", which is more reminiscent of a Victorian parlour than an island croft house. It was like a breath of fresh air to me when I first heard Gaels in Cape Breton and Newfoundland sing it **their way**—usually at the milling boards, full of life, seldom the same way twice.

Allan's Gaelic version (alas, recorded with too many thumps for the CD) was longer than Frank's. Nevertheless, Frank's version not only demonstrates the song's natural evolution but also a better understanding of the meaning than the scholarly professor's 'Nut-Brown Maiden'. [Allan's words, see *The Last Stronghold*.]

CHORUS:
Ho ró mo nighean donn bhòidheach,
Ho ri mo nighean donn bhòidheach
Mo chaileag laghach, bhòidheach
Cha phòsainn ach thu.

1. Cha tèid mi do na bantraich,
   Cha tèid gu dè bheir ann mi
   A Pheigi 's tu bheir ann mi
   'S ann ann tha mo rùn.

2. 'S e 'n t-òl a dh'fhàg gun mheas mi,
   'S e 'n t-òl a bhrist' mo chrìdh.
   Mo thruaigh an tè gheibh mise,
   Bidh uisg' air a sùil.

3. I asked her if she loved me
   She said she was above me;
   She opened the door and shoved me,
   And called me a fool.

4. Ho ro my dark-eyed maiden,
   Ho ri my dark-eyed maiden,
   My bonnie dark-eyed maiden,
   I would only marry you.

Chorus: Ho-row my brown-haired maiden,/ Ho-ree my brown-haired maiden/ My sweet and lovely maiden/ I'll marry none but you.

1. I won't go to the widows'/ I will not, whatever will take me there/ Peggy, it's you who will take me there/ It is there that my love is.
2. Drinking has left me without respect/ And drink has broken my heart/ Pity the one who gets me/ She will have tears in her eye.
3. I asked her, etc.
4. Ho ro, etc.

24. Big John MacNeill Set Trad.
Johnnie Archie MacDonald. Rec. MB, 1970.

Johnnie Archie's first tune is a driving variant of a tune composed by Peter Milne (1824-1908), the talented (if tragic) Scottish fiddler, composer, dancer and teacher. The man for whom Milne made his tune was a famous Highland dancer at the turn of the 20th century.

25. Canntaireachd (learning bagpipe tunes) Trad.
Allan MacArthur. Rec. MB, 1970.

Allan MacArthur explained how he was taught to play the bagpipes via the pipers' ancient syllabic method, canntaireachd. When it came to learning a new tune, he drew a parallel to language acquisition:

> When you know the words [or syllables] and the air, that's just as good as the [printed] notes, pretty near. I couldn't play by note but by ear, you see. For fast tunes, the old tunes, when you know the Gaelic way of it, well, you had the run of it.

Over eighty years of age, and in declining health, he nevertheless demonstrated all in one breath—and concluded: 'and there's a lot of tunes goes a lot easier on your fingers than that tune.'

26. Frank's MacPherson tune Trad.
Frank MacArthur. Rec. MB, 1970. Ref. LS, pp. 142-44.

As a very young boy, Frank (b. 1919) remembered a Scottish piper visiting his father. The visitor was so taken with how well Frank's elder brother Jimmy played that he taught him a tune. The piper was none other than the famous son of the legendary 'Calum Piobaire', Cluny MacPherson's piper, who, when he died (1898) his obituary described him as 'the World's Greatest Piobaireachd Player.'

> Now this John MacPherson, that piper that came here, Jimmy was only nine years old at the time. He was reasonably good on the pipes —in fact, he used to have to put the big drone on the opposite side, you know, put it over his head, because he was small, and using the big pipes! And Jimmy learnt a tune from that man—now I'm not sure that this is exactly the way he played it, and it may not be exactly the way Jimmy used to play it, but it's pretty close. And it goes like this.

27. Canntaireachd for accordion Trad.
Frank MacArthur. Rec. MB, 1990.

Frank, known far and wide as the best step-dancer ever, was also a fiddler and accordion player. Though he didn't play the bagpipes, he demonstrated how the old method could be adapted to playing pipe tunes on other instruments.

28. Canntaireachd (The Smith of Chillichassie) Trad.
Frank MacArthur. Rec. MB, 1990.

This is one of the tunes for which Allan had words, *puirt luath*, as he called *puirt-à-beul*. Frank had the tune, but not the words. Unfortunately my recording of Allan had excessive background noise but here is what he sang:

> Theid mi Cheann Loch Àlainn is fàgaidh mi taobh Loch Obha (x3)
> Sgadan is buntàta ga fhàgail an Ceann Loch Obha.

TRANSLATION:
I will go to Kinlochaline and I will leave the side of Loch Awe/ (x 3)/ Herring and potatoes being left at the head of Loch Awe.

29. Allan on Pipes: Cock o' the North Pipe set Trad.
Allan MacArthur. Rec. MB, 1970.

Though Allan's health was declining and he was becoming very short of breath, he still had impeccable timing for his march and never lost the vitality of his style.

MacArthur's Kitchen Party Dìleab

Ailein Partaidh Cidsin MhicArtair

1. MacArthur's Island Comp. Gordon Cormier
**Gordon Cormier with Loretta Cormier Johnson and
Mallory Johnson.** Album Title: *The Shamrock, Thistle
& Rose*. Produced by Rick Hollet & The Cormiers

From the time the first MacArthur settled beside the
Great Codroy River, they enjoyed one of the most
picturesque views in the Valley. The family home was
built on the hillside overlooking the Great Codroy
River and a beautiful little estuary island, which they used as grazing for
their animals. *MacArthur's Island*, as it became known, was easily accessed
across the tidal sandy isthmus—an idyllic spot for a picnic at haymaking
time.

When Allan and Mary MacArthur's daughter Margaret married Leo
Cormier (whose mother, Lucy, sang in French) the two families shared nine
musical grandchildren. Gordon was seven when I recorded him singing *The
Queen's Maries*, accompanying himself on button accordion; Loretta, aged
nine, sang English and French songs with her sisters Karen and Patricia. Both
have made careers out of music; not only are they part of Newfoundland's
vibrant music scene, but they are also known across Canada for their lively
'down home' music and songs rooted in the Codroy Valley.

1. There's a piper in the valley playing old familiar tunes,
   He marches there below the hill every Sunday afternoon;
   And the people driving by would always stop to hear the sound
   Of a piper marching there upon the ground.

2. Well, his name it was MacArthur and known by one and all,
   As he sang and played at cèilidhs all around;
   He was never short of stories and he'd tell you like it was,
   Just close your eyes and you were Scotland bound.

CHORUS:
 Looking on MacArthur's Island as many a time before,
 Brings back so many memories of home;
 I remember Grandpa telling us of Scotland far away,
 And praying to God he'd make it there some day.

4. He could almost smell the heather rolling from the gentle breeze,
   As his mother told him stories of her home;
   She was born and raised in Scotland, then moved to Newfoundland,
   To live the rest of her life no more to roam.

6. Now the purple heather's growing over on MacArthur's Isle,
   And the house is standing empty on the hill;
   But if you stop and listen carefully, you can almost hear the sound
   Of a piper marching there upon the ground.

         CHORUS: x 2

2. Shamrock, Thistle and Rose Trad.
Frank MacArthur. Rec. MB, 1990. Ref. LS, pp. 188-89.

Haymaking time had all the family in the field, so I happily volunteered
to drive Allan and Mary to over to St Andrew's to have hair-cuts—a day
fixed in my memory not for the home-hairdressing, but for all the old-timers

gathering in Sandy MacIsaac's the moment the MacArthurs appeared. Haircuts? "No, no. We don't see enough of Mary and Allan these days." So began the cèilidh—tea, yarns, tunes, songs, rum, more tea, maybe another glass, and a request for one they all called "Allan's Song". So far I haven't been able to find out the origin of **Shamrock, Thistle and Rose**, but it seems to have a ring of the early twentieth century music-hall about it. As Allan had no English songs from his family, he may have picked up this one in the bunkhouse of a work camp in the state of Maine:

> I went to Bangor, and from Bangor I to Ellsworth, and from
> Ellsworth out to Bar Harbour islands, nine miles out to sea … That
> was 1908. I was working in a tree nursery, lifting Christmas trees …

As this recording of Frank is clearer, here's four verses of the song, a hundred years after Allan may have heard it:

> CHORUS:
> O where is the Scotsman that don't love the thistle?
> And where is the Englishman that don't love the rose?
> Show me the true-hearted sons of old Erin
> That don't love the land where the shamrock grows.
>
> 1. The English they boast of their glorious Nelson
>   And well they may boast of such men
>   For they met and defeated the fleets at Trafalgar
>   And fought on, the brave English boys.
>
> 2. The Scotsmen they boast of their Bruce and their Wallace
>   And well they may boast of such men
>   For they proved themselves true to the thistle and heather
>   Their equals they'll never find again.

3. And long may the English, the Irish and Scotsmen
    United defy all their foes
    And long may they live to possess those dear emblems
    The shamrock, thistle and rose.

3. Oidhche Challainn (New Year Customs) Trad.
Allan MacArthur. Rec. MB, 1970. Ref. LS, pp. 116-17.

Until the 1960s folk celebrated the Twelve Days of Christmas when they had great fun going from house to house in disguise then eating, drinking, singing and dancing. The most special night was Oidhche Challainn when they brought in the New Year, as Allan describes:

> The women and the men and the boys, they'd get together and after supper when it would get dark they would club together now ... like if there were three or four or five from this house, well they would prepare and go to the next house. And when they'd get to the next house, they would start at the door and go right around the house and every one with a little stick in his hand, you know, beating the house. They was driving out the Old Year and letting the New Year in. And it was all Gaelic, you see. And every door they would come to, well when they'd go around the house they would knock on the door, and the woman would be there and she wouldn't let you in if you didn't have a rhyme, or sing. And when you'd be through with the rhyme, you'd come in and they'd offer you a drink of rum or a drink of whisky or something. And then the crowd in that house would get ready and go to the next house. Well, when they'd be crowd enough of boys and girls, and old men with them too, for to

dance, well that's where they would stay. And they would put up a dance, you know, and they wouldn't be short of whisky or rum either. Well that's the way they used to spend New Year's Night [Eve], you know, probably seventy years ago, or something like that.
Slàinte! [Health!] Down the track!

4. Rann Challainn (New Year's Rhyme) Trad.
Allan MacArthur. Rec. MB, 1970. Ref. LS, pp. 115.

> Oidhche chullainn Challainn chruaidh
> Thàinig mise le m' dhuan gu taigh.
> Thubhairt am bodach rium le gruaim
> Buailidh mi do chluais le preas.
> Labhair a' chailleach a b' fhearr na 'n t-òr
> Gum bu chòir mo leigeil a-staigh
> Airson na dh'ithinn-sa de bhiadh
> Agus deuran beag sìos leis.

TRANSLATION:
On a cold frosty Night of the *Callainn* (New Year's Eve)/ I came with my rhyme to a house/ The old man said to me with a frown/ I'll hit you on the ear with a briar/ Said the old woman who was better that gold/ That I should be let in/ For all the little food that I would eat/ And a little drink to go with it.

5. Square Dance Set Trad.
Johnnie Archie MacDonald (fiddle). Rec. MB, 1970.

Not only at New Year but also at house parties, weddings and other social occasions, the very mention of a 'square set' has folk up on the floor forming sets for Quadrilles or Lancers.

6. **Christmas Time Down Home** Comp.

Carol Kriste Messal & Loretta Johnson
Loretta Johnson with Gordon Cormier ,Randall Cormier & Mallory Johnson. Album Title
Christmas Time Down Home. Produced by
Cormiers, 2005.

Allan's grand-daughter Loretta (Cormier) Johnson
has been singing since early childhood. She has a 'heart and soul' way with of
singing that comes across in this song she composed with her cousin. Though
Loretta now lives in St John's, her heart will always be in the Valley.

> CHORUS
> Nothing quite as cheery than to see the dogwood berries
> Bright against the freshly fallen snow
> The pond is frozen nicely for the skaters on the ice
> They're laughing even though it's ten below.
>
> 2. Oh there's nothing anywhere can bring this feeling
>   In fact there's only one place that I know
>   There's nothing anywhere that's quite as healing
>   Like Christmas time down home.
>
> 3. The Northeast wind comes whining but we don't really mind it
>   'Cause Christmas lights have set our hearts aglow
>   I hear the sleigh bells ringing and carollers a-singing
>   Coming through the pines along the road.
>
>   CHORUS: X 2

7. A Chailin Dhuinn Bhon Dh'fhàg Thu Mi Trad., Miss Lyle and reel set Trad.

Margaret Bennett (voice), Martyn Bennett (fiddle) with Jack Evans (guitar). Rec. MB, 1990.

The song being in strathspey rhythm, as often as not a step-dancer would be up on the floor beating out the rhythm with every step. And once the dancers are up, all that's needed is another tune to keep the dance going–then of course the reels.

In the late 1980s and early nineties, along with some of our musician friends, Martyn and I did a series of Edinburgh Festival Fringe events at the Scotch Malt Whisky Society. One of our friends, Jamie MacDonald Reid, was the step-dancer on this occasion, and Martyn's choice of tune is this old strathspey, Miss Lyle. Popular in Cape Breton for 'as long as folk can remember', it is attributed to Captain Simon Fraser of Inverness-shire (1773—1852) who composed and collected tunes in his day.

(See CD 1, track 15 for the text)

8. Calvin's Mandolin set Trad.

Calvin Cormier (mandolin), Sears MacArthur (guitar), and Stan Farrell (spoons). Rec. MB, 1990.

The kitchen has always been the favorite gathering place of family and friends. Teapot on the stove, bottle opener hanging from a string from the fridge door—it's the perfect place for a tune. The kitchen of the old Cormier home, where Allan's grandson Calvin lives, is the setting for this tune. The mandolin was scarcely in Calvin's hand when his Uncle Sears 'just happened' to have his guitar. His brother-in-law Stan grabbed a set of spoons from a kitchen drawer—

"Take it away, boys!"
"Does this tune have a name?"
"Does it have to have a name?" came the droll reply.

9. Will You Marry Me, My Bonnie Fair Lassie? Comp. Murdoch MacArthur
Frank MacArthur. Rec. MB, 1990. Ref. LS, pp. 182-83.

Frank learned this song from his father whose older brother, Murdoch (1878-1961) composed it. He was one of several song-makers in the Valley and was known for his sharp wit, both in Gaelic and English. Another of the brothers, Lauchie, lived about forty miles inland from the family home, in a settlement known as 'Highlands' which features in this song. With wry humour that characterised generations of Gaelic satirists, Murdoch was having fun 'spilling the beans' and teasing Lauchie about a courtship. The transcription here is not precisely as Frank sang it, but is based on Allan's longer version, which Frank heard in childhood.

> CHORUS:
> Will you marry me, my bonnie fair lassie?
> Will you marry me, my damsel?
> Answer me my bonnie fair lassie
> 'S fhad a bha mi fhìn is mi 'n geall ort.
>
> 1. Mi fhèin is Iain Dhòmhnaill 's a' mhadainn moch Di Dòmhnaich
>   Lèine bheag gheal agus tie oirnn
>   Ar dosain air a lìobadh 's ar smig air an sgrìobadh
>   A' falbh chon na gruagaich 's na *Highlands.*

2. Coimhead thus' an dràsda air Mìcheal Iain Bhàin
   Buideal aige làn is dà cheann ann
   Ma thèid thu dhan àite 's a chuireas tu air fàilte
   Glainne bheag 'na làimh bheir e dram dhut.

TRANSLATION:
Chorus: Will you marry me, my bonnie fair lassie (etc)/ It's a long time since we were pledged to each other.
1. Myself and Donald's son Iain, on Sunday morning/ dressed in our little white shirts and ties/ Our hair sleeked back and our chins shaven/ set off to see the lassies up in Highlands.
2. Look now at Iain Bàn's Michael/ He has a full cask, complete with stoppers/ If you go to his place he'll welcome you/ with a wee glass in his hand to give you a dram.

10. Allan on Gaelic 1970 & proverb
Allan and Mary MacArthur. Rec. MB, 1970. Ref. LS, pp. 61.

As he looked back over his life, Allan reflected on when he first started school: 'I was nine years old, and I couldn't understand a word of English… I'd know 'yes' and 'no', that was all.' Before long, however, he was as fluent as the monoglot teacher, because the education system shared the same policy that dealt a death-blow to Gaelic in Scotland: to appoint English-speaking teachers to make sure Gaelic would be supplanted. Nevertheless, Allan and Mary MacArthur raised their eleven children entirely in Gaelic, knowing full well they would pick up the other language as soon as they went to school:

Allan: In the home, well, up till about five years ago we never spoke
English in the house; everybody talked Gaelic.

Mary: Oh yes.

Allan: And then when company'd come in it was Gaelic.

Mary: They all spoke Gaelic

Allan: But now, there's no Gaelic now. Mun d' thuirt e: *'Bhon chaill mi a' Ghàidhlig na b' fheàrr cha d' fhuair mi'.*

TRANSLATION:
As he said: 'Since I've lost the Gaelic language nothing better have I found.'

11. Òran an t-Saighdeir (The Soldier's Song) Trad.
Allan MacArthur. Rec. MB, 1970. Ref. LS, pp. 177-78.

Though there are many recruiting songs in Scotland, I can find no trace of this one. Allan, whose brother wore a kilt when he joined a Highland regiment at the outbreak of the First World War, told me:

> Well, you had to be over six feet or else you wouldn't be taken in the *Rèisimeid Dhubh* (the Black Watch). They were pressing them you know—you had to go. They would examine you and if you were the height and everything, you were physical fit, there was no getting out of it. They used to call it *racruitear*—I don't know what they calls it in English. [recruitment]

> CHORUS:
> Hù a hó tha mi fo lionn-dubh
> Hug órann ó mi trom gu dìreadh
> Hù a hó tha mi fo lionn-dubh.

1. 'N oidhche bha mi aig a' mhuileann
   Thruis a' chuideachda mum thimcheall.

2. Chuir iad an t-òr dearg nam phòca
   Chan e mo chòir bhith ga innse.

3. Chuir iad an it' àrd nam bhoineid
   Bha siud dorranach le m' mhuinntir.

4. Thoir mo shoraidh-sa gum mhàthair
   Bho 's i 's cràiteach dh' fhàg mi 'n tìr sin.

5. Dìreadh ris a' charra chreagain
   Tha mise 'n eagal nach till sinn.

6. Dìreadh ris na Beanna Siùbhrach
   Donnchadh Bàn 's a chùl ri dhìlsean.

TRANSLATION:
Chorus: Hù a hó, I am in distress/ *Hug órann ó*, heavy-hearted climbing to the top of the hill/ Hù a hó, I am distressed.
1. The night I was at the mill/ The company gathered around me.
2. They put the red gold in my pocket/ I am ashamed to tell it.
3. They put the tall feather in my cap/ That was vexing for my people.
4. Take my blessing to my mother/ As she is the saddest I left there.
5. Climbing the craggy hill/ I fear we won't return.
6. Climbing the hills of Jura/ Duncan Bàn has his back to his kindred

12. The Miracle of Christmas Comp. L & M. Johnson, G. Cormier & C.K. Messal
Mallory Johnson with Loretta Johnson, Randall & Gordon Cormier.

Album Title: *Christmas Time Down Home.*
Produced by Cormiers Entertainment
Inc.

Allan's grandmother knew of Highland
soldiers who fought in the Battle of
Waterloo (1815), as during her lifetime
over 10,000 soldiers from Skye fought in the Napoleonic campaigns. Then,
not only his mother, but also Allan himself, lived through the time when
Canada (the 'neighbours') sent over 8000 soldiers to the Boer War (1899).
Not surprisingly, there were many memories in Allan's household of loved
ones who fought in World War I and the next generation in World War II—
especially the 'boys' who never came home.

Every war has its songs, with poets, song-makers and singers
becoming the voices of conscience for their kinsfolk. In the present day,
the devastation of the Iraq War makes Newfoundlanders ask 'Why should
our soldiers die?' Newsreel reports invade kitchen table conversations,
even *cèilidhean*, pressing responsibility on song-makers, not just to sing of
the heartache, but also to keep hope alive for those in the shadow of the
bombing. This song (voted SOCAN Song of the Year, 2007) grew out of a
conversation approaching Christmas when everyone prayed for the safe
return of Canadian troops. Allan's great-grand-daughter Mallory Johnson
(Lorettta's daughter) sings lead, her clear voice and youthful conviction
bringing hope for every soldier's safe return.

1. It's a cold winter's night, snow softly fallen,
   Fire in the kitchen keeps her warm
   She heard it on the news today, another one is gone,
   But there's been no knock upon her door,

2. He hasn't called to let her know he's made it out alive,
   But deep down inside her heart she knows
   Her soldier's coming home.

3. She believes in the miracle of Christmas
   She's seen it happen many times before,
   As she looks out the window, down that long winding road,
   She knows her soldier's coming home.

4. She longs to see his footprints in the freshly fallen snow
   It was Christmas Day when he walked out that door
   It seems like only yesterday, but a year has passed her by
   Since he left to fight an unforgiving war

5. Repeat verse 2 and 3

6. End with verse 3

13. Ailean Duinn (Brown-Haired Allan) Trad.
Margaret Bennett with Seylan Baxter (cello).
Ref. LS, pp. 165. Album: *Take the Road to Aberfeldy.*
Produced by Grace Note Publications

A pensive moment of reflection on Mallory's song about war brings me back to the unknown composers of the war songs Allan learned from his mother— *Òran an t-Saighdeir* and this one, *Hù a hù Ailein Duinn*, which I learned from Allan. No matter how many generations pass since the songs were made, or the wars fought, the emotion endures. These songs—and soldiers—deserve to be remembered. (For the text, see notes *MacArthur Cèilidh* CD 1- track 5)

14. Tullochgorm Trad.
Sears MacArthur. Rec. MB, 1990.

One of the finest button-box players in Newfoundland, Allan's son Sears is now in his seventies. He's much in demand for cèilidh's and a great favourite with dancers.

15. Making Moccasins and songs—The whole story
Allan MacArthur with John, George and Martin. Rec. MB, 1970. Ref. LS, pp. 167-68.

MB: Your brother [Murdoch] composed it, did he?
Allan: He made the moccasins himself, you know, out of cowhide. You had to stretch the cowhide (after you'd kill the animal) on a wall or something, till it was dry. And then you would cut out the strip around eight inches wide and twenty-four inches long and then you'd scrape the hair off it with a sharp knife or even with glass …
John: You had to tan it too.
Allan: Oh yes.
MB: How did you tan?
Allan: Birch bark, oh yes. We used to take that off o' the trees, you know, in June and July when the sap would be outside of the wood, next to the bark. It was no trouble to peel the bark off in big

slices, probably that long [3 feet], and probably 12 inches wide or something like that. And you'd dry it, and then you'd take the rough off o' the outside and you'd plane it, you know, with the plane to make it smooth leather from the green hide to go into [the tanning solution]. Of course, you'd have to soak the hide first, you see. You'd split it in the centre and put it in a great big puncheon and put the bark onto it and water, and that's the way. Leave it for a few days, probably four days the first time, then you'd throw the water away and throw all the bark away, set it in again you know, and the third time you'd leave it probably for a fortnight and the leather would be tanned then, you see, fit to use. You'd make shoes out of that—tap leather [for soles] and everything else.

John: It would stain the leather brown.
Allan: Oh, yes, yes,
MB: When did you stop tanning leather?
Allan: Well, I suppose it's twenty-five years since I didn't tan any leather.
MB: And this song was the one your brother made about it?
Allan: About the moccasins, well yes, Murdoch composed it … and he had a lot more verses too.

16. Òran nam Mogaisean (The Moccasin Song) Comp. Murdoch MacArthur

Allan MacArthur with sons George, Martin and John. Rec. MB, 1970. Ref. LS, pp. 166-67.

Already seated at the kitchen table, Allan had no sooner sung his first note than he and 'the boys' took hold of the tablecloth, thumping it vigorously on the table to keep time in their improvised milling:

CHORUS
Tha fonn, fonn, fonn air,
Tha fonn air na mogaisean,
Tha fonn gun bhith trom,
Hog i ó air na mogaisean.

1. Thòisich Seumas Ryan
   'S rinn e craicean do mhogaisean,
   Gun chairt e dhiubh na h-adhbrainn
   'S cha robh iad craobhaidh fhathast air.

2. Thèid mi sìos don aifhrionn
   An coibhneas nan caileagan,
   Cha ghabh iad facal ùrnaigh
   Ach sùil air mo mhogaisean.

3. Fhuair mi craiceann caorach
   'S dùil rium caol a ghearradh às,
   Thilg mi 'n dara taobh e
   Ach fhuair mi laoicionn gamhnach.

TRANSLATION:
Chorus: Let's sing, sing, sing, sing Let's sing about the moccasins/ Our song won't be heavy/ Hokey-ho for the moccasins!
1. James Ryan got started/ With a piece of hide for the moccasins/ Although he tanned the ankle leather/ They weren't yet soft enough.
2. When I go down to mass/ In the company of the lasses/ They can't say a word of prayer/ For staring at my moccasins.
3. I got a piece of sheepskin/ To cut a strip from it/ I tossed it to one side / But found a calf-hide.

17. **Òran nam Mogaisean** (The Moccasin
    Song) Comp. Murdoch MacArthur, music
    by Martyn Bennett

Martyn and Margaret Bennett. Album Title: *Glen
Lyon: A Song Cycle*. Produced by Martyn Bennett
2002.

From when I first met Allan MacArthur, it was evident
that, whatever else our families shared—language,
music, culture, a good cup of tea, hearty laughter—we also shared a passion
for handing on tradition.

"The home is where it all begins," we would agree.

Twenty-five years later (and back home in Scotland), my son Martyn
planned an album of songs featuring five generations of our family in
Skye—his great-grandfather, Peter Stewart (recorded 1909), down to his own
generation. He asked me to sing 'family songs', but took me by surprise by
adding to my list *Òran nam Mogaisean*. But this is from Allan MacArthur's
family! "So? I've known the MacArthurs and that song all my life!" And so
I sang it.

On reflection, he was only a babe in arms when Allan's wife, Mary,
lulled him in her rocking chair. The following summer she delighted to
have him call her 'Grandma MacArthur', though she already had a host of
grandchildren. The youngest would play with him and the older girls (Karen
and Carina in particular) would mother him, sing with him and take him
with them on summer days or come with us on outings. And so, between
the MacArthur household and our own, Martyn thought everybody sang,
played music, danced, and gathered in the kitchen on a Saturday night.

Though Allan died before Martyn was a year old, Frank continued to sing it and everyone would join the chorus. There were countless opportunities to hear songs and play music till, at the end of each summer, my 'little fieldwork assistant' and I would head for St. John's. At the archives of Memorial University we'd make copies of the tapes, take them home and listen to them over and over again. That's what every folklorist has to do to transcribe recordings. While training be a folklorist, I also learned this: *Never underestimate the influence of what your child hears, even if you think your little game is just to keep him out of mischief while you work!* 'You press the button when I say STOP. Wait for REWIND…now GO!' This may have begun Martyn's early fascination for recording machines and technology, but it was not till we recorded *Òran nam Mogaisean* that I realized the incredible detail he had absorbed during those years. I think Allan MacArthur would have shared my astonishment to hear *Òran nam Mogaisean* travel the world via Martyn's CD *Glen Lyon*. That said, Allan should have the last word, for only he, Murdoch and their generation knew the Mi'kmaq families whose skilled leatherwork they admired—the last of the Codroy Valley's Mi'kmaqs returned to Nova Scotia in the 1940s.

18. Last word on moccasins Trad.
Allan MacArthur. Rec. MB, 1970.

This little ditty concluded Allan's discussion on moccasins and songs. I suspect it's not easy to sing with tongue so firmly in cheek, but Allan MacArthur could do it more convincingly than most! "Where did you learn that?" I asked. "Oh, my mother could sing that too—it'd be no trouble for a MacIsaac to learn that sort of thing!" He looked me straight in the eye, giving away nothing in his expression, while 'the boys' waited for a response, grinning from ear to ear.

19. **Cock Your Leg Up** Trad.
Frank MacArthur. Rec. MB and Kenneth Goldstein , 1980.

Many a Saturday night waltz has been danced round MacArthur kitchens to this tune. What about the name? 'Well,' said Frank, 'it don't make much sense to me—but you can sing it too!'

> Cock your leg up, cock your leg up, cock your leg up old horse,
> Cock your leg up, cock your leg up, cock your leg up old horse!

20. **Allan's Tongue Twister** Trad.
Allan MacArthur. Rec. MB, 1970.

Gather round children, now, try saying this fast!

> Cha robh reithe leathann liath riamh reamhar!

TRANSLATION: A broad grey ram was never fat.

21. **Dèan Cadalan Sàmhach** (Sleep peacefully) Trad.
Allan MacArthur. Rec. MB, 1970. Ref. LS, pp. 179-80.

Allan's mother sang this version of an old lullaby that is also associated with Gaelic settlers in North Carolina and Nova Scotia. From as far back as he could recall, it was one of her favourite songs when nursing her ten children, born between 1887 and 1895. The last time Allan heard her singing it was in the 1930s when she was spinning. It's the right rhythm for that too, you know, because she had no babies then!

CHORUS:
Dèan cadalan sàmhach a chuilein 's a rùin
Fuirich mar tha thu 's thu 'n dràst' an àit ùr
Tha òganaich againn làn bheairteas is chliù
Bidh tusa nad oighre air feareigin dhiubh.

1. 'S ann an Ameireaga tha sinn an dràst'
   Fo dhubhar na coille nach teirig gu bràth
   Dar dh'fhalbhas an Dùldachd 's a thionndaidh am barr
   Bidh measan 's bidh ùbhlan gu dlùthar a' fàs.

2. 'S truagh nach robh mis' ann an dùthaich MhicLeòid
   Far an d'fhuair mi òg m' àrach nam phàiste glè òg…

TRANSLATION:
Chorus: Sleep peacefully, my pet, my love/ Stay as you are, you're now in a new place/ We have young men full of riches and renown/ You will be the heir to one or other of them.
1. We are now in [North] America/ Under the shade of the endless woods/ When the winter goes and the crops change colour/ Berries and apples will be growing abundantly.
2. Pity I was not in the land of MacLeod/ Where I was reared as a very young child…

22. Daddy's Little Girl Comp. Vanessa MacArthur
Vanessa MacArthur with Max Piercey, Barry Musseau and Corey Anderson. Album Title: *MacArthur Drive.*

Allan MacArthur's eldest son, Lewis, and his wife Jessie raised ten sons and a daughter who all had Gaelic. There was plenty of music and dancing among them, though on this collection only Leonard plays, as he happened to be around at the time. Vanessa's father, Hugh, played mandolin, was a good dancer and very light on his feet—a gentle giant with an infectious MacArthur smile, he was immensely proud of his Gaelic heritage. Alas, Hughie was only in his fifties when told he had cancer, and very little time left. Within a few days of this devastating news, Vanessa wrote her beautiful, heart-rending song, which she later recorded on her first album, *MacArthur Drive*. She chose her title because 'Hugh MacArthur had more *drive* than anyone I have ever known.'

> He was a strong man, a super father, a wonderful friend, and the most gentle soul I've ever met. I remember growing up, Dad would speak small phrases of Gaelic and eventually I learned them, and there could not be anyone more proud— his daughter speaking a few small words of Gaelic. And the first time I played the bagpipes for him, big and strong as he was, he cried like a baby! So, knowing that I was singing on this wonderful project would have him in tears.

> 1. He would never rescue me, he'd teach me to find my way
>   He always let me make my own mistakes
>   He'd show me how to stand, stand up on my own
>   And he'd be there to catch me when I fall.
>   I am trying so hard, Daddy,
>   To be strong for you and for me
>   Now I'm holding your strong shoulder, Daddy
>   It's time to grow up for Daddy's little girl.

2. And I just can't believe you're leaving me this way
    My heart is breaking for one last time;
    Poppy's little boys will grow to know what a man you were,
    They're the ones who'll be missing most of all
    And I am trying so hard, Daddy (etc)

Repeat, part B, with last line:

I love you Daddy, from your little girl.

23. Miss Rowan Davies Comp. Phil Cunningham
Martyn Bennett and Gordon Cormier. Rec. G. Cormier, 1988.

Musicians usually like to share stories of where they got their tunes, and though I wasn't there to record this magical afternoon, thankfully Gordon reached for a cassette recorder. In July 1988 there was a big family gathering—relatives from out west, the Maritimes, Ontario, California, everywhere! It was Loretta's wedding and, though invited, we had to send regrets with our good wishes from Scotland. But Martyn decided he'd surprise them—turn up, kilt and all, and he'd pipe the newly-weds out of the church. What a surprise, what a wedding present! For days afterwards, every MacArthur and Cormier household was filled with those who stayed on to visit. Martyn was in his element, and so was his lifelong friend, Allan's grandson, Gordon. (Just for the record, they played their first concert together, and there's a faded newspaper clipping to prove it—Gordon aged seven, Martyn just three.) Gordon takes up the story: 'Sitting on Mom and Dad's front porch playing tunes, trying new arrangements of old ones, learning new—this is one that Martyn came up with,' which Gordon accompanies so naturally.

Though I first heard it on Phil Cunningham's album *Airs and Graces* (1984), Martyn's own best memories were of playing the tune with Phil who lived on the Isle of Skye—or, in Phil's words, *"Martyn was about thirteen or fourteen— Rowan would be about five at the time—and he would walk miles over the hills, Glenconon to Flodigarry, carrying his bagpipes, just to play tunes!"* And so the admiration and affection for Phil's step-daughter, Miss Rowan Davies (and his tunes), reached the Codroy Valley via a penny whistle and a wedding.

24. Tips Eve Jig Comp. Gordon Cormier
Gordon Cormier. Album Title: *Christmas Time Down Home*. Produced by Cormiers Entert. Inc. 2007.

When you choose another time of the year to go home, make sure it's Christmas. And if you get home to the Valley the night before Christmas Eve (Dec. 23) you'll be there for 'Tips Eve'—that's what they call it around here.

25. Remember Home Comp. Don & Peter Brownrigg
Don Brownrigg. Album Title: *Wander Songs* Produced Weewerk Records, 2007.

Don's first solo album, produced in Halifax has received critical acclaim. This reflective song (composed with his uncle) is apt for all young folk who leave their native land. Though Don now lives in Halifax, the Codroy Valley will always be home.

1. You turned and said that you'd be leaving
    I didn't really know what to say
    'Cos you've been around for such a long time
    I'd grown to hope that you were going to stay.
    I realize there's nothing here to hold you,
    And that makes my words so much harder to say —

2. Yes, you are a man and you life belongs to you
    You have to make the best of things no matter what you do
    Remember fights and people's wives are to be left alone
    And if all else you fail you, please, remember home.

3. Hello, son, so good to hear you!
    Where are you now and tell me how you've been;
    I hear you've done an awful lot of growing;
    Have you grown enough to handle what you're in?
    Hello, son, so good to hear you!
    It's good to hear you sound so in control;
    It's too bad you couldn't make it home for Christmas
    How's the wife, married life and little Nichole?

4. Yes, you are a man and your life belongs to you
    You have to make the best of things no matter what you do
    Remember fights and people's wives are to be left alone
    And if all else you fail to do, please remember home.
    It's hard to believe the things I'm hearing
    Harder still to learn that they are true?
    It's not the first time that you've been faced with trouble,
    Now you're by yourself, what will you do?

5.   Yes, you are a man and your life belongs to you
     You have to make the best of things no matter what you do
     Remember fights and people's wives are to be left alone
     And if all else you fail to do, please remember home.

26. Cha Dèan mi 'n Obair Trad.
Martin MacArthur & Margaret Cormier. Rec. MB, 2006.

Regardless of the years, or decades, since Allan's death, his life, songs and music still feature in every kitchen gathering, house party, birthday, anniversary, wedding or wake connected to the MacArthur family. Home on holiday from Alberta in 2007, Allan's son Martin (now in his eighties) still step-danced to the fiddle and was 'up for a waltz' at the very sound of 'Come on, Uncle Martin!' He and his sister Margaret laughed as they remembered their father singing this one—'probably somebody'd had a few homebrews!'

> Cha dèan mi 'n obair, cha dèan mi 'n obair,
> Chan urrainn dhomh 'n obair a dhèanamh
> Chan òl mi deoch, 's chan ith mi biadh
> Chan urrainn dhomh 'n obair a dhèanamh.

TRANSLATION:
I won't do the work/ I won't do the work/ I can't do the work/ I won't drink a drop, I won't eat a bite/ I can't do the work

27. Nach do Ghoid mi 'm Piatan Trad.
Martin MacArthur. Rec. MB, 1970.

'This is just another one I heard from my father,' Martin laughed.'Now this

Mìchael lived over in Loch Lomond; and Mòr, now she was a Campbell. You know, just for fun he'd sing it. No harm meant at all!'

> Nach do ghoid mi 'm piatan a bh'aig Mìcheal?
> A sheinn e, sheinn e na chadal
> Horo dn-ho, hn-dri-ri-ri
> Rn-dorro, hn-dorro hn-dorro,
> Mòr Chaluim, Mòr Chaluim

TRANSLATION:
Did I not steal Michael's little pet lamb?/ He sang, he sang that in his sleep/ Hn-dorro, hn-dorro [bagpipe imitation]/ Morag, Malcolm's daughter, Morag, Malcolm's daughter.

28. MacArthur's Kitchen Party Comp. Gordon Cormier and Òran na Caillich Comp. A. MacDougall

The Cormiers; Rec. album 2007; **Allan MacArthur & friends.** Rec. MB, 1970. Ref. LS, pp. 181-82. Album Title: *The Cormiers Comin' Home*. Produced by Cormiers Entertainment Inc.

Only someone who had been to many a MacArthur *cèilidh* or kitchen party could have created a song with such vividness it is almost like a documentary. These are real mandolins and fiddles, real homebrew, real singers, musicians and dancers who know how to keep their traditions alive. And, as if no cèilidh could take place without one of his songs, the track includes part of Allan's version of *Òran na Caillich* with his old friends thumping a lively chorus. The song, which Allan learned from his own mother, was composed in the late 1700s by the bard Allan McDougall, *Ailean Dall* (blind Allan), of Glencoe. Allan sang five verses (three of which became part of this track) then added, 'and the one who composed it was never married himself, although he gave the poor woman such a calling down!' Meanwhile, Allan's own wife, Mary, sat knitting as he sang—a more gentle, caring and kindly woman would be hard to find. As Frank put it, 'We were so lucky,' for it was Mary who made the tea and baked bread, cakes and cookies, and whose warm smile made everyone glad to be around them.

1. We're having a kitchen party at MacArthurs' tonight
   And anyone who's anyone you're welcome to invite
   Bring along your fiddle and good ol' pair of shoes
   And we'll crack the cork of another keg of Uncle Johnny's brew.

2. Well here come the MacDonald boys with mandolin and fiddle
   And a tall guy with reddish hair is standing in the middle;
   He sings a cappella and what a sound he can produce
   Sure everyone here knows him well, he goes by Bill the Bruce.

3. Just get your duds in order and when your work is done
   Get all your friends together, tell everyone to come
   Tonight we're gonna raise the roof, we'll all be there at nine
   The cèilidh's at MacArthurs', we'll be having a helluva time!

4. So many conversations, people talking up a storm;
   Margaret sings in Gaelic like her father before.
   No trouble to tell the Scotsmen for they're singing every song
   It matters not the age you are to keep tradition strong

5. Aunt Mary's telling stories of cèilidhs long ago,
   The friends that she remembers are long since gone, you know.
   You can almost see them dancing there and stepping on the floor,
   With all the noise they're making sure you'd never hear the door.

6. Just get your duds in order …(etc. as verse 3)

FIDDLE BREAK (*in 'square set tempo'*) **Cock o' the North,
Òran na Caillich:**
1. Nuair thig mi bhon chrann an àm an earraich,
   Le fuachd air mo chàil, 's mi 'n geall mo gharadh,
   Chan fhaod mi na taing dol teann air an teallach
   Mum buail i gu h-ealamh le bròig mi.

CHORUS:
O hì o hà, gur cruaidh a' chailleach,
O hì o hà, gur fuar a' chailleach,
O hì o hà, 's i ghràin a' chailleach,
Dh'fhàg mise nam amadan gòrach.

2. Cha dèan i dhomh feum, 's cha ghrèidh i aran,
   Cha 'n àraich i feudail, sprèidh, no leanabh,
   A' laighe 's ag èirigh 's ag èigheach 's a' gearan,
   'S gun reicinn gu deimhinn air gh ròt i.

3. Mur ceannaich mi 'n tì cha d' fhiach mi m' earraid
   A leigheas a cinn, 's i tinn a' gearan ;
   Cha dèan i rium sìth, ach strì is carraid,
   'S ri cànran teallaich an còmhnaidh.

TRANSLATION:
Song for the Ol' Woman
1. When I come in from ploughing in spring/ I'm cold right through and looking forward
   to getting warmed/ I'm not allowed to get anywhere near the hearth/ In case she gives
   me a swift kick with her boot.

Chorus: Oh hee-oh-hah, how hard the old woman is/ …how cold the old woman is/ …I'm disgusted with the old woman/ Who made me out to be a stupid fool.

2. She's no use to me / and she won't knead bread/ She won't raise livestock, cattle or a baby/ Going to bed and getting up she's shouting and complaining/ I could gladly sell her for a groat.*

3. I'm no use to her if I don't buy tea/ To heal her head when she's sick and complaining/ She won't make peace with me, only strife and conflict/ And she's forever grumbling.

NOTE: *A groat is an old Scots coin, scarcely worth a dime.

29. Deoch Slàinte; Lord Lovat's Lament Trad.
Allan MacArthur. Rec. MB, 1970.

Allan loved to raise his glass to the company with a favourite toast:

> *Deoch slàinte a' chuairtear a ghluais à Albainn!*
> Here's a health to the traveller who left Scotland!

One of the last tunes he ever played (as breath began to fail) was **Lord Lovat's Lament**. Although it is popular as a pipe march, Allan's generation also sang it as *Fuadach nan Gàidheal*, one of the most poignant songs about eviction and exile from Scotland.

Let's raise a glass to the traveller who never saw Scotland—
Allan MacArthur!

Margaret Bennett,
Ochtertyre, 2009

Acknowledgements

I will forever be grateful to Allan and Mary MacArthur for their warm welcome, generosity and friendship. Through four decades the entire MacArthur family and several branches of it have shared hospitality, music and kinship—my heartfelt thanks goes to all of them, the Cormiers, MacIsaacs, MacDonalds, MacNeils, Farrels, O'Quinns and Johnsons. The four generations of singers and musicians who have so willingly contributed to these recordings are:

1st. Allan MacArthur, his wife Mary and brother-in-law Johnnie Archie MacDonald.
2nd. Allan's children: Frank, George, John, Margaret (Cormier), Martin and Sears MacArthur.
3rd. Allan's grandchildren: Leonard MacArthur, Helena and Brendan MacArthur, Calvin, Karen, Loretta and Gordon Cormier.
4th. Allan's great-grandchildren: Vanessa MacArthur, Mallory Johnson and Randall Cormier, Don Brownrigg.

A huge debt of gratitude is due to Professor Herbert Halpert (1911—2000), founder and head of the Folklore Department of Memorial University, who taught me, believed in me, encouraged me—like Allan MacArthur, he still inspires me. The late Dr. John Lorne Campbell of Canna also helped me via his correspondence, and in 1996, after John's death, his wife Dr. Margaret

Fay Shaw generously invited me, with three of Allan MacArthur's family (daughter Margaret and grand-daughters Karen and Loretta), to spend a week on Canna—we will never forget the experience or her generosity.

During my four decades of fieldwork recordings I have appreciated the co-operation and assistance of many colleagues: at Memorial University of Newfoundland, the Folklore Archive staff made CD copies of my original reel-to-reel tapes; at Edinburgh University the late Fred Kent, sound-archivist at the School of Scottish Studies, his successor Stewart Smith, along with Dr. John MacInnes and Dr. Hamish Henderson, generously shared friendship as well as expertise; and in Glasgow sound technologist Bob Whitley of the RSAMD helped with the studio master. In Perthshire, special thanks go to my husband, Gonzalo, not only for his encouragement and love, but also for the countless hours he worked on design and layout, scanning photos, editing tapes and making tea. Having shared two wonderful visits to the Codroy Valley with me, he knows it's worth it!

My parents, George and Peigi, deserve a very special mention—my father introduced me to the Gaelic speakers of the Codroy Valley in the first place, and later visited with me many times. With Allan he shared unbridled enthusiasm for piping, canntaireachd and dancing, which gave an important dimension to our visits. And, from her first meeting with Allan and Mary, my mother exemplified the 'true Gael'; over the years she has been a stalwart support, particularly in helping me with Gaelic transcriptions and translations.

During this project I also appreciated Catriona Murray's translation of the introduction and several helpful discussions on proofs with Bill Innes, Jamie MacDonald and Brendan MacArthur. Over several versions, my long-time friend and proof-reader Marie Salton kindly rescued me from several textual errors, though any that crept back in are entirely my own

I wish to thank the Scottish Arts Council for helping to fund my visit in 2007 (enabling me to record additional Gaelic songs), the Foundation for Canadian Studies in the United Kingdom and the Gaelic Books Council for financial assistance towards the production of *Dìleab Ailein—Allan's Legacy.*

Finally, my gratitude goes back a lifetime to my grandparents, who taught me 'the old Highland ways' by the example they lived, and my parents and sisters who shared their songs and music with warmth and love. Most of all, I treasure the time spent with my son, Martyn, my constant companion in the Codroy Valley from 1971—75. As enthusiastically as he shared songs and music with me, he also shared childish curiosity and enthusiasm to explore barns and stables, feed animals, ride on top of hay carts and on winter sleighs. In his teens, he transcribed all the melodies of Allan's songs for my book, *The Last Stronghold*, sharing my hope that others may enjoy Newfoundland's rich heritage of Scottish Gaelic tradition.